THE
OLD BANK

THE
ROCHESTER SAVINGS BANK

THE
OLD BANK

THE
ROCHESTER SAVINGS BANK
AND ITS
PRESIDENTS AND TRUSTEES
FROM
1831 TO 1983

James C. Duffus

RIT PRESS

Published and distributed by
RIT Cary Graphic Arts Press
90 Lomb Memorial Drive
Rochester, New York 14623-5604
http://carypress.rit.edu

ISBN 978-1-933360-41-6

Library of Congress Cataloging-in-Publication Data

Duffus, James C., 1927-
    The Old Bank: the Rochester Savings Bank and its presidents
and trustees
from 1831 to 1983/James C. Duffus.
        p. cm.
    Includes bibliographical references and index.
    ISBN 978-1-933360-41-6 (alk. paper)
    1. Rochester Savings Bank–History. 2. Banks and banking–
    New York
(State)–Rochester–History. I. Title.
    HG2613.R64R63 2009
    332.2'10974789–DC22

                                2009043158

CONTENTS

DEDICATION

To Dancy, Adair, Sarah, Tom and Nell

PREFACE

This book chronicles the 152-year life span of a truly great Rochester
institution, the Rochester Savings Bank. It was a mutual savings bank that,
by definition, was owned by its depositors and operated for their benefit.
At one time, there were more than 4,000 savings banks in the u.s.,
most having started in the 1800s. By 1990, many of these had disappeared.
They had accomplished what they were created to do, and eventually
they fell prey to changing economic times.

Rochester Savings Bank was a bulwark of strength in Rochester, New York
for 152 years. Its presidents and trustees were key figures in the life of a
city that grew from a wilderness town of the early 1800s to become one of
the fastest-growing cities in America. The bank's trustees played a major role
in the beginnings of the University of Rochester and the establishment of
the Rochester Institute of Technology–two of Rochester's great stabilizing
institutions. Four bank trustees were the founding members of the University
of Rochester and many more have served on its board. Over 40 trustees have
served as RIT trustees since its founding. Ten of its trustees, including me,
served as board chairs of another influential community stabilizer–the YMCA.

The bank's ultimate association with the Royal Bank of Scotland (the fifth
largest bank in the world) was a triumphant ending to a long odyssey followed
by few other banks. RSB's journey spanned the years of the development of
the u.s. banking system as well as the beginning and near end of the highly-
regulated mutual savings bank era in the u.s. Given the current financial
environment, one can't help speculating about the possible resurgence of
savings banks in this country.

My association with (and passion for) the Rochester Savings Bank began in the summer of 1943 when, at age sixteen, I served as its messenger. Seventeen years later, I was invited to become the youngest trustee in the history of the bank. I spent 34 years on the RSB board and on the board of its successor. During that time, I saw firsthand the competitive problems that began, roughly, in the 1960s, and continued on through the merger with Community Savings Bank in 1983. I was privileged to serve with many Rochester business leaders, including four different Eastman Kodak Company CEOs and three different Xerox CEOs, as well as with the man who wrote the first U.S. Social Security legislation in the 1930s. My seat at the board table had been held by George Eastman. This was pretty heady stuff for a young man!

Jim Duffus

Acknowledgments

The following individual organizations and sources contributed mightily to my preparation of this work and I thank them all.

The Department of Rare Books and Special Collections, in Rush Rhees Library at the University of Rochester, houses the archives of the Rochester Savings Bank, courtesy of Citizens Bank. Special thanks belong to Nancy Martin, the John M. and Barbara Keil University Archivist and Rochester Collections Librarian at the University of Rochester, and to Richard Peek, director of the library's Department of Rare Books and Special Collections and Preservation, both of whom were immensely helpful to me.

At the local level, I would like to thank the City of Rochester Historian Christine L. Ridarsky, and City Photographer Ira Srole, and the Rochester Public Library, Local History Division. I am also indebted to the Rochester Historical Society, the George Eastman House, the Rochester Museum and Science Center, The Landmark Society of Western New York, and Adair Duffus Mulligan, editor of the Lyme, New Hampshire *Historian*.

I appreciate the help of Joseph Hammele, the Executive Vice President of Rochester Savings Bank at the time of its merger with Community Savings Bank, and Executive Vice President of Rochester Community Savings Bank after the merger.

Many thanks to RIT's Cary Graphic Arts Press: David Pankow, director; Molly Q. Cort, managing editor; Amelia Hugill-Fontanel, assistant curator; and Marnie Soom, design and marketing specialist. In addition, I am grateful to Becky Simmons, RIT archivist; Bruce Ian Meader, professor of graphic design and Elizabeth Lamark, visual resources manager at The Wallace Center.

Dane Gordon, Professor Emeritus of RIT's College of Liberal Arts, was of inestimable help in the preparation of this work. He is a prolific author, his latest publication by RIT's Cary Graphic Arts Press being *Rochester Institute of Technology, Industrial Development and Educational Innovation in an American City, 1829–2006.*

I am also grateful to William P. Albert, public relations manager at the Harris Beach law firm, and Ruby Morse, former president of the Rochester Female Charitable Society. Special thanks belong to Gilman Perkins, Jane Gorsline, Jane Steinhausen, William Morse III, and Mitchell Pierson Jr., for providing ancestral pictures. Also thanks to Edward Pettinella for his advice and insight.

RSB seal

RSB seal

CSB logo

RCSB logo

Charter One logo

CHAPTER ONE

SETTING
THE STAGE

One of Rochester's truly great historic institutions, the Rochester Savings Bank (RSB), began operations in 1831 with a $13 deposit. By September 2004, RSB was part of a larger bank, with assets of $42 billion, which was then acquired by the fifth largest bank in the world, the Royal Bank of Scotland, for $10.5 billion cash. "The Old Bank," as the Rochester Savings Bank was affectionately called, enhanced the lives of Rochesterians for over 150 years through its support of many cultural and civic institutions, including, among others, the Rochester Institute of Technology, the YMCA, and the University of Rochester. This history of RSB follows many of the twenty presidents and some of the 153 trustees who served the community during the lifetime of this longstanding financial institution. RSB's life cycle corresponds closely to that of savings banks in the United States during this period.

RSB existed in Rochester as one continuous unaltered entity for 152 years, from the day it was chartered by New York State, April 21, 1831, until July 1, 1983, when it merged with Community Savings Bank, becoming the Rochester Community Savings Bank. Community Savings Bank was the product of a 1944 merger of East Side Savings Bank, organized in 1869, and Mechanics Savings Bank, incorporated in 1867. The only other savings bank in town, Monroe Savings Bank, incorporated in 1850, failed on January 29, 1990.

At the time of the merger, the new Rochester Community Savings Bank (RCSB) had assets of $2.4 billion and was the fifteenth largest mutual savings bank in the country. Three years later, the bank's charter was changed from a mutual savings bank to a publicly-held stock institution. RCSB raised $184 million in capital and brought its net worth to $290 million. Another merger followed in 1997 with Charter One Financial, Inc., of Cleveland, Ohio.

In September 2004, Charter One Financial, whose total assets had reached $42 billion, was acquired by the Royal Bank of Scotland for $10.5 billion in cash. The Royal Bank of Scotland, chartered on May 31, 1727, is one of the world's oldest, largest and most prestigious banking institutions. At the end of 2007, it ranked fifth in the world with assets of $1.9 trillion. With 226,400 employees, the Royal Bank of Scotland serves forty million customers in fifty-three countries. Its U.S. holding company, Citizens Financial Group, known locally as Citizens Bank, had $161 billion in assets at the end of 2007, and is the ninth largest U.S. bank, ranked by deposits. These are significant numbers compared to the Rochester Savings Bank's first deposit of $13 made in July, 1831. For me, this history has come full circle since my great grandfather emigrated from Scotland in 1831.

Flour Mills at the Genesee River Falls

CHAPTER TWO

THE ERIE CANAL
AND THE
FLOUR CITY YEARS

Chartered in 1817, the village of Rochesterville, population one thousand, became part of the County of Monroe in 1821. Just four years later, the Erie Canal opened (1825), followed by the opening of the Rochester Savings Bank (1831), and the chartering of the City of Rochester (April 1834). The Erie Canal triggered an immense boom in Rochester, comparable to the 1849 Gold Rush in California. Canal boatmen, migrants and rapid urban growth put a huge strain on the community's stability. A carnival atmosphere prevailed for the drifting laborer.[1]

Erie Canal

---

1 Blake McKelvey, *Rochester on the Genesee: The Growth of a City* (Syracuse: Syracuse University Press, 1973), 33, 40.

Genesee Falls and Sam Patch's Platform

Stuntman Sam Patch's leap over Rochester's "Upper Falls" of the Genesee River was the climax of Rochester's chaotic 1820s. While many early inhabitants left the area during this time, there were good men and women who stayed and helped create a more balanced society. After an 1830 religious revival led by the Presbyterian minister Charles G. Finney (who later became the president of Oberlin College), there was a demand for institutions that would encourage and support working men and their families. Finney promoted industry and thrift, and RSB was founded on these virtues.[2]

During the 1820s and 1830s, Rochester had the fastest-growing population in the country. To the west, even to the shores of the Pacific, there was no city of equal size, except possibly Cincinnati.[3] By 1835, eighteen flour mills were clustered around the falls of the Genesee River, grinding 460,000 barrels of flour a year. Rochester was nicknamed the "Flour City," since the flour industry drove the economy from 1834 to 1854.[4] Improvements to the mouth of the Genesee River helped expand the import of Canadian wheat and the development of the mills.

---

2 Gerard E. Muhl, "Paying for the Dreams: A Short History of Banking in Rochester," *Rochester History 49*, No. 2 (April 1987), 5.

The Flour City years were boom years for Rochester. Both millers and merchants prospered. They built impressive homes in the Third Ward, or the "Silk Stocking Ward," as it was known in the 1820s and 1830s. The Campbell-Whittlesey house at 123 S. Fitzhugh Street and the magnificent Hervey Ely house on the corner of Troup Street and Livingston Park still stand today. William Kidd, RSB President from 1860 to 1865, would later reside here.

Campbell-Whittlesey House

Hervey Ely House

Rochester's urban population grew rapidly, but was bottom heavy and unstable, with over three quarters of its residents under the age of thirty. In 1828, there was one imprisoned debtor for every ten families, a telling example of the conditions of the day and the need for reform.[5] At the time, the city had only two small commercial banks, the Bank of Rochester (1824–1846) and the Bank of Monroe (1829–1849). These banks catered strictly to commercial interests, not to individuals, so there was no place where the average citizen could safely deposit his or her savings. Rochester Savings Bank was born in the midst of this scene.

3 Jack Speare, Editor, ed., *In Rochester 100 Years Ago and Now: Centennial Year of the Rochester Savings Bank, 1831–1931* (Rochester: Rochester Savings Bank, 1931), 19.

4 Henry O'Reilly, *Sketches of Rochester*, (Rochester: William Alling), 361.

5 Gerard E. Muhl, *Rochester History*, 49, No. 2, (April 1987), 5.

RSB's fifteen founding fathers had great foresight. As men of prominence and means in the small but rapidly-growing community, they pushed to establish a savings bank that would encourage thrift and personal discipline. The bank's charter petition to the state stated,

"There is no reason for a resident of a Rochester boarding house to hoard money where thieves may break in and steal or where it will be subject to the common risks that pertain to keeping cash in the ordinary hiding places in dwelling houses."[6]

Perhaps because it expressed such a clear reason, the charter petition was accepted in only two years, overcoming the opposition of the two established commercial banks in Rochester, and several older and larger ones in Batavia, Geneva, and Canandaigua. All were apprehensive of what they regarded as an invasion of their territory, even though they weren't interested in this kind of retail business.[7]

On April 21, 1831, the New York State legislature chartered the Rochester Savings Bank in perpetuity. It was the sixth savings bank in the state, and the first one chartered west of the Hudson River. It survived completely intact with an unblemished record for 152 years, when it merged with Community Savings Bank. During its first seventy years, many banking institutions opened and closed in Rochester. Specifically, forty-eight local banks (savings, commercial, private and savings and loan) were formed from 1828 to 1900.[8] They were somewhat loosely regulated, and only a very few survived the financial ups and downs of that period. Those that did survive were merged or acquired, and remain part of the Rochester banking scene today: J. P. Morgan Chase Bank, the Bank of America, HBSC Bank, M&T Bank, KeyBank and Citizens Bank, the direct descendant of RSB.

---

6 Susan T. Turri, *The Rochester Savings Bank, 1831–1981:*
   In Commemoration of Its 150 Years of Service
   (Rochester: Rochester Savings Bank, 1981), 8.

7 Susan T. Turri, *The Rochester Savings Bank, 1831–1981,* 8.

8 Gerard E. Muhl, "Banks of Rochester through 1900,"
   Unpublished paper, CA 1980, Rochester Historical Society.

During its first seventy-five years of existence, "The Old Bank" endured four major national financial panics, in 1837, 1857, 1893 and 1907, and several minor ones. RSB also persevered through a run on the bank in 1878, the Civil War, two World Wars, the 1929 stock market crash, and the Great Depression.

Another stabilizing but little-known Rochester institution, the venerable Rochester Female Charitable Society began before RSB and is still very active.[9] Established in the Spring Street home of RSB founding trustee Everard Peck in February 1822, the Society was quietly dedicated to doing "good works."

Everard Peck House

9 "Rochester Female Charitable Society," River Campus Libraries, University of Rochester, http://www.library.rochester.edu/index. cfm?page=1109.

Among its many charitable endeavors were founding the Rochester Orphan Society (1837), now known as Hillside Children's Center, the City Hospital (1847), now Rochester General Hospital, and the Home for the Friendless (1849), now The Friendly Home. The RFCS also founded the Industrial School of Rochester (1857) which became Rochester's Children's Nursery, known today as Rochester's Childfirst Network. In 1919, in response to World War I, the organization created the Visiting Nurses Association and the Medical Motor Service. There were sixty charter members of the Rochester Female Charitable Society, twenty-one of whom were related in one way or another to RSB. The first RFCS president was Elizabeth Ward, the wife of Dr. Levi Ward, RSB's first president. Other members included Everard Peck's wife, Chloe, and his daughter, Emily. Throughout the years, society members have included descendants of these sixty founding ladies as well as many relatives of RSB trustees.

New
Bank Poster

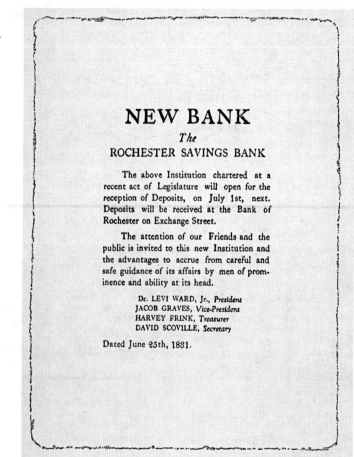

NEW BANK
The
ROCHESTER SAVINGS BANK

The above Institution chartered at a recent act of Legislature will open for the reception of Deposits, on July 1st, next. Deposits will be received at the Bank of Rochester on Exchange Street.

The attention of our Friends and the public is invited to this new Institution and the advantages to accrue from careful and safe guidance of its affairs by men of prominence and ability at its head.

Dr. LEVI WARD, Jr., *President*
JACOB GRAVES, *Vice-President*
HARVEY FRINK, *Treasurer*
DAVID SCOVILLE, *Secretary*

Dated June 25th, 1831.

Dr. Levi Ward

Everard Peck

Two weeks after the RSB charter was approved, on the evening of May 10, 1831, an organizational meeting of the fifteen founding trustees was called by Dr. Levi Ward, Everard Peck and Jonathan Child. These men, leaders in the civic and commercial affairs of the young city, were especially representative of all the trustees over the 152-year lifespan of the bank. They elected Dr. Levi Ward as the first RSB president.

Dr. Ward, a physician, was truly one of Rochester's pioneers. A Yale graduate, he came to the village of Rochesterville in 1817 and was, from the first, a respected leader. Until nearly the time of the Civil War, he habitually wore black knee britches and black slippers with prominent silver buckles, attire worn by only a few other citizens. Dr. Ward was also one of the founders of the Bank of Rochester (1824–1846), the village's first commercial bank, and became its second president. At the time, it was legal for commercial and savings banks to share officers, and until 1979, they could also share directors. These institutions were long considered non-competitive, although after World War II this situation changed. Dr. Ward helped launch the Athenaeum, the seminal forerunner of the Rochester Institute of Technology (RIT), and he was one of its first seventeen directors. Through the years, over forty RSB trustees were involved with RIT.

Everard Peck, another key founding trustee, was a printer, bookseller and bookbinder. He left the printing business in 1831 to become a banker. In 1850, he was one of the founding trustees of the University of Rochester (U of R), established in large measure because of him. Peck held many of the U of R's early organizational meetings in his home. His wife's brother, John N. Wilder, was the university's first board of trustees' president.

Like Peck and Dr. Ward, many other RSB trustees made significant contributions to the life of Rochester by helping to start and/or support such stabilizing community assets as RIT, the U of R, and the YMCA. Today, the U of R, with its huge medical center, is Rochester's largest employer, with over 18,000 employees. RIT ranks eighth among private sector employers, with 3,400 employees. A 2007 article in the AARP (American Association of Retired Persons) Magazine, entitled "Linking the Generations," ranked RIT as one of the nation's 50 best employers of workers over 50. In the same article, Rochester's YMCA was ranked fourth (Cornell University was first), ahead of such prestigious institutions as MIT, Harvard and L. L. Bean. Over the years, ten RSB trustees were board chairs of the YMCA, and many more were directors.

Jonathan Child

Child's father's tavern at Lyme, NH

Another important RSB founding trustee, Jonathan Child, was born in Lyme, New Hampshire, where his family owned a tavern on the Connecticut River. When Child was twenty-one, his father gave him a saddle horse and $100, which was the custom of the time. He migrated to Utica and taught school for five years. Having saved $100 of his pay, he sold the horse, sent the money back to his father, and moved west to Rochester.[10] As we shall see, Jonathan Child had an aversion to alcohol which may have stemmed from what he witnessed in the tavern days of his youth.

---

10 William F. Peck, *Semi-Centennial History of the City of Rochester* (Syracuse: D. Mason, 1884), 686–87.

Child married a girl named Sophia Eliza, the eldest daughter of Colonel Nathaniel Rochester, the founder of Rochesterville. Three years later he became an agent for the first successful shipping company on the Erie Canal. He went on to establish the Pilot Line, which had the largest number of boats (thirty-four) on the canal. Jonathan Child was a valued citizen, respected by the community and beloved by his friends and family. In 1834, at the age of forty-nine, he was the aldermen's choice to be the first mayor of Rochester. By 1900, fifteen other RSB trustees had served as mayors of the City of Rochester.

Child weathered the financial Panic of 1837 by converting some of his canal boats into coal carriers, becoming the city's first coal dealer. He built Child's Basin on the canal in the heart of Rochester, which quickly developed into the most active harbor in town. It extended north on the west side of the Genesee River aqueduct between present-day Exchange and Aqueduct Streets, about where the statue of Mercury now stands.

A year after he was elected mayor, the city council disagreed with his efforts to control liquor licenses, and Child resigned. He turned his attention to the construction of the classic colonnaded house still standing on Washington Street that looks down to where the Erie Canal once flowed. Five Corinthian columns grace the front portico of this most imposing mansion that, for many years, was a center of fashionable life in Rochester. While many parties and balls were held there, no liquor was ever served. After Mrs. Child's death in 1850, the mansion was occupied for two years by John Wilder, president of the board of trustees of the newly established University of Rochester (U of R). Many of the university's early functions took place behind the home's stately pillars.

Childs Basin on the Erie Canal

Jonathan Child House

Another original RSB trustee, David Scoville, was a merchant. When the bank needed someone to handle deposits and other paperwork, Scoville resigned as trustee and became the bank's financial secretary, on July 1, 1831. His annual salary was $300, and for fifteen years, he was the bank's only employee. Every Saturday evening he sat at a window set aside for RSB in the old Bank of Rochester (the city's first commercial bank) on Exchange Street. The window was also open one mid-week evening each month "for females only."

RSB's first customer, a grocer and baker named Harmon Taylor, deposited $13 on July 2, 1831. His passbook showing that transaction is archived in the Department of Rare Books and Special Collections in Rush Rhees Library at the U of R.

RSB first bank window

The first fifteen trustees were respected men in the community, recognized leaders who were willing to serve the new bank without pay. One of them, Ashbel Riley, was a carpenter who came to Rochester in 1816 and helped build the area's first high school in 1827. During a cholera epidemic, he stepped in to fill a vacancy on the Board of Health. Not only did Riley serve without pay, he also personally buried most of the town's 118 victims while helping to care for others in a makeshift hospital. In 1825, he was in charge of a militia regiment that was selected to escort the Marquis de Lafayette on his journey from Rochester to Canandaigua. Riley was later promoted to Major General. An avid temperance man, Riley almost eradicated drinking from his regiment. One of his hand bills read: "One thousand able-bodied men wanted to hear an address on behalf of drunkards' wives and children, by General Riley." He gave 400 lectures in Europe and many more in the U.S. Riley paid for medals and gave over 6,000 of them to people who would take "the pledge."

First RSB deposit by grocer Harmon Taylor

In 1831, Isaac Hills became the first RSB elected (as opposed to founding) trustee. A lawyer, Hills played a large part in organizing Rochester's city government. He was one of the original proponents of RSB, and had drawn up its charter application in 1829. Hills became RSB's secretary and, in 1880, its president for a year. Elected mayor in 1844, Hills was an important leader of the bank and the community during both the "Flour City" and "Flower City" years.

Jacob Gould became an RSB trustee in 1832. Born in Boxford, Massachusetts, he moved to Rochester in 1819 and became a successful shoe manufacturer. In 1835, he was selected by the city council as the second mayor of Rochester. (Mayors were elected by popular vote after 1840.) Governor DeWitt Clinton appointed him major general of artillery and he escorted the Marquis de Lafayette on his tour of Rochester in 1825. Presidents Jackson and Van Buren appointed him Customs Collector, and President Polk appointed him U.S. Marshall in 1845. He became a U of R trustee in 1854.

Isaac Hills

Jacob Gould

Thomas A. Rochester   *Abraham Schermerhorn*

Thomas A. Rochester, the sixth child of Colonel Nathaniel Rochester and the first of his children to settle in Rochester, became an RSB trustee in 1833. As the sixth mayor of Rochester, from 1839 to 1840, he had a hard time weathering the aftermath of the Panic of 1837. That national financial crisis cast a pall on his mayoralty, ultimately ending his political career.

In 1824, Abraham Schermerhorn came to Rochester after graduating from Union College. He became the cashier (an important position in those years) of the commercial Bank of Rochester, and an RSB trustee in 1834. Schermerhorn was known as the "money king" of the Genesee region. When a loan that he had granted to the Eagle Tavern went sour, his bank wound up owning the city's leading tavern/hotel in a foreclosure proceeding. Today the Powers Building is on the site of the Eagle Tavern. Schermerhorn was named Rochester's third mayor in 1836, but he left after two months for the more lucrative post of secretary to the New York State Senate, and served two terms in Congress.

Charles Hill

Charles J. Hill became an RSB trustee in 1836. He had been taken in at the age of twelve by a lawyer's family in Woodbury, Connecticut, and as a result was a well-educated young man. However, he chose trade over law, and came to Rochester in 1816. Hill became a trustee of Rochesterville in 1822, and the city's mayor in 1843. A remarkably industrious miller, his "Hill Flour" product was a favorite in New York, New England and even England. The first World's Fair in London exhibited "Hill Flour" in the Crystal palace in 1851. Hill built the first brick house in Rochester on South Fitzhugh Street. In 1884, William F. Peck wrote, "Mr. Hill possessed those sterling traits of character which the sons of New England carried with them and developed in the West–germs of usefulness, honor and success."[11]

During RSB's first eleven years, the fledgling bank was faced with the Panic of 1837 and its aftermath. A steep drop in wheat prices was attributed to an oversupply of wheat. Although the Second National Bank of the United States had been formed in 1816 to financially stabilize the country, President Andrew Jackson felt that a national banking system was unconstitutional, and, in 1836, he vetoed a bill to renew the bank's charter. This paved the way for wild banking speculations, and bankruptcy became the order of the day. Within a year, the country's banking system suffered a general collapse, with 343 out of 850 banks closing. However, Dr. Levi Ward's effective leadership as RSB's president brought the institution successfully through these challenging times.

---

11   Peck, *Semi-Centennial*, 659–61.

In 1839, the city of Rochester opened a soup kitchen in the shadow of City Hall, and almost 1,400 people were on relief. Although many left the city looking for opportunity in the West, others arrived to take their places, and as a result, the population almost doubled during RSB's first ten years, from 12,000 to 23,000. This continuous influx of people strengthened Rochester's capacity to withstand the decline in the grain trade, because immigrants introduced new specialties to the marketplace. Many commercial banks suspended interest payments to their depositors during these years, and many merchants were forced into bankruptcy. However, RSB never failed to open its single window at the Bank of Rochester,[12] and in the summer of 1842 it moved to its new two-story building at 47 State Street. RSB also never failed to pay interest on its deposits, which clearly demonstrated its resilience and financial security during a difficult period.

First Bank Building at 47 State Street

---

12 Turri, *Rochester Savings Bank*, 11.

William Pitkin

Two trustees were elected during the latter years of Dr. Ward's presidency. The first of these was William Pitkin, a merchant who was elected an RSB trustee in 1838. His wife, Louisa Rochester, was the twelfth child of Colonel Nathaniel Rochester. Although Pitkin built her a gracious home at 474 East Avenue, she declined to move in, apparently because she preferred living in a "more proper" residence in the "Silk Stocking" Third Ward. Pitkin subsequently sold the East Avenue house to Daniel Powers, of Powers Building fame, and today it is the local Boy Scouts headquarters. After four years as a trustee, Pitkin became the second president of RSB, from 1842 to 1849. He was also elected mayor of Rochester in 1847, and became a founding trustee of the U of R.

Pitkin Home

Elijah F. Smith   *John Allen*

In 1841, Elijah F. Smith was elected an RSB trustee. He went on to serve thirty-nine years on RSB's board and become its president three separate times. He was also the first popularly-elected mayor of Rochester in 1840, and was a founding trustee of the U of R. Elijah Smith's wholesale grocery company, Smith and Perkins, became one of the most substantial businesses in central New York.

Two other trustees were added to the board in the 1840s. The first, John Allen, was elected an RSB trustee in 1842, and Rochester mayor in 1845. His is one of the only sad stories in the history of RSB trustees. Allen was a leader in the Irish community, as well as a popular leader of the local militia. However, his term as mayor was not distinguished and he fell into financial misfortune. The month after his term expired his furniture was at auction. Three years later, he received an appointment as tender of an Erie Canal mud lock. Eleven years later, he apparently committed suicide.[13]

George Mumford became an RSB trustee in 1845 and served for twenty-seven years. An 1824 graduate of Union College, he came to Rochester and joined the law firm of Frederick Whittlesey. Mumford & Whittlesey became one of the leading law firms in western New York. Mumford served as RSB's bank attorney for five years, from 1847 to 1852, and also as RSB president for a short time in 1865. He was the president of Traders Bank in 1859, and then became a director and president of Manufacturers Bank. Many mergers later, those surviving institutions became part of today's M&T Bank.

---

13 McKelvey, "Rochester Mayors Before the Civil War"
    Rochester History 26, No. 1 (January 1964), 10.

CHAPTER THREE

THE FLOWER CITY
AND THE
CIVIL WAR YEARS

In the mid-nineteenth century, Rochester was prosperous: "on a roll," so to speak. Elijah F. Smith served two of his three terms as RSB president from 1850 to 1858, and 1859 to 1860. Smith was very influential in the life and growth of both the bank and the community during this period. He retired from his very successful grocery business, Smith & Perkins, in 1859, and for the remainder of his life he concentrated on serving the community. William F. Peck's 1908 *History of Rochester and Monroe County, New York* explained that Smith's "name was ever a most honored one on commercial paper and his business integrity was entirely unassailable...[He] figured prominently in community affairs, contributing in substantial measure to the growth and progress of the city along many lines."[14]

During these years, Genesee River water power was turning more mill wheels than ever before, and canal trade was at a new high. The city was evolving as a result of its increased reliance on steam, the rise of corporate capital, and the efforts of labor to organize. Newly-expanded markets enabled Rochester to transition from a regional milling and commercial center to a more diversified industrial city. In the midst of this prosperity, however, a second national economic depression was brewing.

In the years following the Panic of 1837, New York had been the first state to adopt a comprehensive system for chartering banks and requiring minimum reserves to back circulating notes issued by individual banks.[15]

---

14 Peck, *History of Rochester and Monroe County, New York,
from Earliest Historic Times to the Beginning of 1907*
(New York, Chicago: Pioneer, 1908), 677–78.

15 Turri, *Rochester Savings Bank*, 27.

However, overall regulation by other states was minimal. Western wildcat banks in the non-state territories were completely unregulated and issued unreserved bank notes, hoping that customers would never redeem them. This was a root cause of the Panic of 1857. Within that year, more than 5,000 American businesses failed. British investors lost confidence in U.S. banks and withdrew their money. Gold poured into the economy and helped inflate the currency. Grain prices fell when the Crimean War ended and Russia re-entered the marketplace. Railroad land speculation ruined thousands of investors. While commercial banks in Rochester were severely hurt during the Panic of 1857, RSB actually raised its deposit interest rate from 5 percent to 6 percent and increased deposits by over $140,000. Deposits had increased 800 percent since 1842. The bank moved into a new landmark building on the southwest corner of Main and Fitzhugh Streets in 1857. Twenty-one years later, in 1878, this building had to be enlarged, a testament to the banking leadership of Elijah Smith, the RSB trustees, and their collective and individual involvement in the growing city.

*New
bank building*

*Enlarged
bank building*

Hamblin Stilwell

Hamblin Stilwell became an RSB trustee in 1850. In the late 1820s, he had come to Rochester as manager of an Erie Canal packet boat agency. The same year he joined the RSB board, he also began to serve as commissioner of the new Mount Hope Cemetery. Some say that this appointment might have been a political stepping stone for him because he became Rochester's mayor in 1852. However, a cholera scourge darkened his mayoral term and Stilwell left the city, apparently to escape the epidemic. He was sharply criticized for this perceived abandonment. Friends blamed his behavior on severe illness, while others cried, effectively, "Chicken!"[16]

William Kidd also joined the board in 1850, and became RSB's president in 1860. He developed the Rochester Car Wheel Works, one of the city's most successful businesses. Kidd was also the treasurer of Monroe County. He left Rochester in 1865 to establish a banking firm in New York City.

RSB's building became home to many of the city's cultural and civic organizations over the years, sometimes rent-free. Among them were the Rochester Athenaeum and Mechanics Association (the forerunner of RIT), the Rochester Art Club, the Rochester Historical Society, the Rochester Chamber of Commerce, and the Rochester Club. It was here that artist J. Guernsey Mitchell designed the statue of Mercury–a Rochester landmark for over one hundred years.

---

16 McKelvey, "Rochester Mayors," 15–16.

William Reynolds

Rochester's designation as the "Flour City" eventually gave way to its fame as the "Flower City," from 1855 to 1875.[17] At a time when seed companies, nurseries, orchards and vineyards were springing up across the country, William A. Reynolds and Michael Bateman of Rochester started the Rochester Seed Store. Reynolds became an RSB trustee in 1852. His role in Rochester history as a pioneer of the nursery and seed business came to fruition when two employees, George Ellwanger and Patrick Barry, purchased the nursery portion of the business. Nurtured by the warming effect of nearby Lake Ontario, the Ellwanger and Barry Nursery became one of the most innovative and prosperous enterprises in the country.

*Reynolds
Arcade*

---

17 www.en.wikipedia.org/wiki/history_of_rochester_new_york, 3.

Abelard Reynolds

Inside Reynolds Arcade

In 1845, Reynolds assumed control of Rochester's downtown Reynolds Arcade, which his father, Abelard Reynolds, had built at a cost of $30,000 in 1829. The four-and-a-half-story building had been an instant commercial success, with 350 occupants in its 86 rooms. For many years it was the most important architectural structure west of Albany, and the center of business and professional life in Rochester.

In 1834, the city's first mayor, RSB trustee Jonathan Child, was inaugurated in the Reynolds Arcade. The Western Union Company was also established there. After 104 years of operation, the Reynolds Arcade was found to be a fire hazard in 1932, and had to be razed. A ten-story art deco office building was built on the site and was named the Reynolds Arcade in honor of the original building.

On June 12, 1829, Abelard Reynolds and RSB's first president and founding trustee, Dr. Levi Ward, helped found the Rochester Athenaeum and Mechanics Association (RIT) in the Reynolds Arcade building. Abelard's son William became a chief patron of the Athenaeum. William Reynolds was closely associated with the U of R as well, and was named a university trustee in 1870.

Another RSB trustee elected during the pre-Civil War era was Thomas Kempshall, who joined the board in 1857. His brother Willis had been a founding RSB trustee in 1831. Thomas married the sister of another RSB founding trustee, Everard Peck. Thomas Kempshall owned the very successful Aqueduct Mill, located on the Erie Canal and facing Child's Basin in the center of the city. He had become Rochester's mayor in 1837, and later, a member of Congress. He played on the first Rochester Baseball Club in 1858 at the spry age of 64. In its early years, the game of baseball moved much more slowly than the way it does today, and the rules were quite different. RSB's trustee minutes reflect this tribute to Kempshall upon his death on January 14, 1865:

> "He was one of our oldest citizens in age and citizenship. Few have been more widely, better or more favorably known. He acted no unimportant part in changing a petty hamlet, rude and uncultivated and seated in the primeval forest into the City of Rochester. He has enjoyed riches and endured poverty, seen prosperity and adversity, a good and true man, a patriotic and faithful citizen."[18]

Aqueduct Mill

---

18 RSB trustee minutes, February 6, 1865.

Roswell Hart   *James Brackett*

Roswell Hart, another influential RSB trustee, was elected in 1861 and served for twenty-one years. A graduate of Yale and holder of a law degree, he headed Rochester's first retail coal yard. He and many RSB trustees supported the YMCA because of the stabilizing influence it had in the community. Ten RSB trustees chaired the YMCA board, including Hart, who was the Y's fifth chair. During the presidency of Ulysses S. Grant, Hart was appointed superintendent of the Railway Mail Service for the states of New York and Pennsylvania. He also headed the Rochester Board of Water Commissioners, which built the city's first water system in the 1870s. Hart enjoyed politics and served one term in Congress, from 1865 to 1867. His sister was married to another (future) RSB trustee, Mortimer Reynolds.

A few other key RSB trustees were elected during the early 1860s. James Brackett joined the board in 1862. He came to Rochester in 1838 and established the wholesale firm of Brackett & Averill. When oil was discovered in Western Pennsylvania, Brackett invested in an oil well and became president of the Pennsylvania Tubing and Transportation Company, an early pipeline venture that made him a small fortune. He was known as "The Colonel" because of his activity as the head of the City Dragoons in the mid-1850s. Brackett became the mayor of Rochester in 1864, and RSB president from 1882 until his death in 1904.

Addison Gardiner

Addison Gardiner was elected to the RSB board in 1863. He was a law partner of RSB trustee Samuel Lee Selden. Gardiner, Selden, Thomas Kempshall and future RSB trustee, Charles Pond, played with Rochester's first amateur baseball team, the Flower City Baseball Club, in 1858. They were called clubs, not teams at this time. Gardiner, at 61, was not a young man, nor were most of the other players. Baseball had just been "discovered" by the elite and it was the sports rage of the day. Gardiner later became the chief judge of the New York State Court of Appeals. His grandfather, Isaac Gardiner, had been killed at the start of the American Revolution, on April 19, 1775, in Lexington, Massachusetts.

The country was now embroiled in the Civil War. During this period, RSB was a pillar of the city of Rochester and of the Union. The bank loaned $100,000 to Monroe County for military bonuses. RSB took heavy allotments of government bonds even when the fortunes of the North looked bleak.[19] When the war ended, the strength and stability of "The Old Bank" had brought it safely through one of the most challenging periods in the nation's history. RSB was able to faithfully serve a city whose population had grown from 23,000 in 1842 to 50,000 in 1865.

19 Speare, *Rochester 100 Years Ago and Now*, 35.

American banking changed dramatically as a result of the Civil War. Hard-pressed for cash, U.S. Secretary of the Treasury Salmon P. Chase convinced the federal government in 1863 to charter national banks, an idea that had been tried twice before and abandoned. Up to this point, all U.S. banks had been regulated by the states. The Federal Legal Tender Act of 1862 and the National Bank Act of 1863 enabled nationally-chartered banks to issue their own currency as long as it was backed by holdings in U.S. Treasury bonds. Thus, a national currency was established,[20] resulting in the creation of a dual banking system: the Office of the Comptroller of the Currency was established to charter and regulate federal banks, and individual states continued to charter and regulate their own banks. The next major change in the U.S. banking system would occur in 1913, with the establishment of the Federal Reserve System.

Hollister Home

Emmett Hollister joined the RSB board in 1867. Hollister's father had founded the Hollister Lumber Company in 1832, and Emmett succeeded him in the business, which was the oldest lumber company in Rochester. In 1863–64, he built his large family a home at 207 South Plymouth Avenue, where it still stands today. Hollister was among the ten RSB trustees to chair Rochester's YMCA board.

---

20 Turri, *Rochester Savings Bank*, 28.

Mortimer Reynolds

Reynolds Home on Spring Street

RSB trustee William A. Reynolds' brother, Mortimer F. Reynolds, joined him on RSB's board in 1869. Mortimer developed a paint and linseed oil business which he sold in 1872 so that he could administer the large estates of his older brother William and his father, Abelard. In 1884, Mortimer incorporated the Reynolds Library, donating the 12,000 volumes he had purchased from the old Athenaeum to it, and generously funding a perpetual endowment. These books formed the nucleus of the library's collection, a few of which are now in the Melbert B. Cary Jr. Graphic Arts Collection at RIT. In his 1884 history of the city of Rochester, William Peck wrote, "When the stately figure of the last surviving child of the pioneer Abelard Reynolds [i.e., Mortimer Reynolds] shall be seen no more upon the streets of Rochester, a grateful city will perpetuate the memory of an extinct race."[21]

Atkinson Home

21 Peck, *Semi-Centennial*, 694–95.

Edward Harris   *Harris Home*

Edward Harris, elected a trustee in 1870, became RSB's bank attorney in 1879. In 1850, fifteen-year-old Harris emigrated from England, and was hired as a law clerk the following year by Henry Ives.[22] In 1856, Harris was named a partner in the Harris & Ives law firm, which eventually became the Harris Beach law firm, whose relationship with the bank lasted more than 100 years. Harris built a house in 1867 at 1005 East Avenue in Rochester, and it is still standing today. The extended Harris family was closely involved with RSB for many years, and there would be three people named Edward Harris who served as trustees and bank attorneys.

Hobart Atkinson, elected a trustee in 1871, became RSB's president in 1904. Born in Rochester in 1825, he married Louise Sibley, daughter of Hiram Sibley, the co-founder of the Western Union Company. Within two decades of its incorporation, Western Union would become the largest corporation in America. In 1871, Atkinson and his second wife (Louise died in 1868) acquired the property at 484 East Avenue, which became and until recently remained the home of the Rochester Historical Society. Atkinson, a charter member of the venerable Genesee Valley Club, became its president in 1885, when the club's annual dues were only $50.

---

22 "Harris Beach Law Firm Looks for Historical Anecdotes to Celebrate," *Daily Record* (Rochester, NY), October 24, 2005.

During Trustee Elijah F. Smith's third term as RSB president (from 1872 to 1880), another financial panic struck the country, with a stock market crash on Black Friday, September 20, 1873. Once again, RSB's reputation for stability brought increased deposits at a time when many in the city were suffering unemployment and hardship.

George J. Whitney, the son of a leading Rochester miller, Warham Whitney, became a leading grain merchant himself, and also a member of the RSB board in 1872. Building a huge grain elevator in 1857 led to his gaining absolute control of all the grain that passed from Buffalo to New York City on the New York Central Railroad. As a director of the New York Central, he knew Cornelius Vanderbilt quite well. Whitney became a private banker in 1871, but he had to close that endeavor due to over-extending himself during the stock war between Jay Gould and Cornelius Vanderbilt. A number of other Rochester businessmen were caught up in the stock war and, unfortunately, at least two of them shot themselves.

John Williams

Gilman H. Perkins (center, seated)

John Williams also became an RSB board member in 1872. He came to Rochester in 1824 as a miller's apprentice and soon acquired his own mill. In 1833, he married Caroline Whitney, daughter of Warham and sister of George Whitney. After her early death, he wisely married her sister Olive, which cemented his partnership in Whitney's lucrative enterprise. Active in politics, he was easily elected the mayor of Rochester in 1853, and was considered the strongest mayor of the decade.

Gilman H. Perkins was elected a trustee of RSB in 1879. He is seated in the center in the Perkins family picture. Since 1853, Perkins had been a business partner with RSB president Elijah Smith's wholesale grocery house, Smith and Perkins. The Perkins home on East Avenue became Rochester's Genesee Valley Club in 1922.

Another RSB trustee elected in 1879 was Charles Pond. An 1860 alumnus of the U of R, he was the third oldest living graduate at the time of his death at age 93. He practiced law, went into the milling business, and then returned to his law practice. Pond served for fifty years on the boards of Rochester General Hospital, Rochester School for the Deaf, and Hillside Children's Center. He was city comptroller from 1907 to 1913, and a member of Rochester's Flower City Baseball Club.

During the first few days of 1878, RSB had its first and only "run" after a disgruntled preacher started a rumor that the bank was unsound. It was quickly squelched when two trustees went to New York City and brought back $1 million in cash, which was prominently displayed at the bank.[23]

Perkins Home (presently the Genesee Valley Club)

---

23 Joseph Hammele, "Early Banking in Rochester," presented to RIT's Institute of Fellows, September 15, 2003.

CHAPTER FOUR

THE MATURING YEARS: THE CITY OF MANY INDUSTRIES BECOMES THE HOME OF QUALITY PRODUCTS

The 1880s found Rochester with abundant skilled manpower and investment capital. Into this environment came men of ideas who catapulted the city into national prominence. As East Avenue mansions continued to be built, Rochester's wealth filtered down to the surprised working men, who found themselves becoming homeowners and voracious consumers. The population in Rochester increased from 50,000 in 1865, to 130,000 in 1890. More than half of the population was under the age of twenty-five, and so the face of the city was very youthful. Thus began a twenty-year period when Rochester was often referred to as "The City of Many Industries." [24]

Kimball Tobacco Company

---

24 Turri, *Rochester Savings Bank*, 33.

William S. Kimball

Along with Perkins and Pond, William S. Kimball, a key figure in late nineteenth-century Rochester, was also elected to the RSB board in 1879. A successful entrepreneur, his Kimball Tobacco Company was the largest cigarette manufacturer in the country. The factory was located on what was formerly an island in the Genesee River, approximately on the site of today's Blue Cross Arena.

*The
Mercury
Statue*

George Eastman would later purchase the factory and its island, and lease it back to the city at no cost. The building later served as a City Hall annex for many years until the construction of the Community War Memorial, which is now part of the Blue Cross Arena. Kimball commissioned his brother-in-law, artist J. Guernsey Mitchell, to design a statue of Mercury, the symbol of commerce. The design was completed in 1881 in Mitchell's studio on the third floor of the RSB building. Some said that Kimball wanted such a public statue to counteract Victorian social leaders who believed that cigarettes were a decadent French product.[25] At 162 feet high, the Mercury statue has graced the Rochester skyline for many years, first on top of the Kimball factory building and, since 1974, on the nearby Aqueduct building.

Bathers

Kimball was known as a great salesman. One of his ideas that worked especially well was placing a bathing beauty playing card in each pack of cigarettes. With enough purchases, smokers could collect a free deck of bathing beauty playing cards. Kimball was named a U of R trustee in 1892. His home (now gone) stood next to 139 Troup Street, and it exemplified the opulence and eclecticism of the Gilded Age.[26] At one time, Kimball was considered to be the wealthiest man in Rochester, and his home contained what many called the most beautiful art gallery in the country. It was surrounded by a lovely garden–he was especially devoted to raising orchids. After visiting Nantucket Island in 1892 and playing his first round of golf there, Kimball and four friends brought the game to Rochester, and helped to establish the Country Club of Rochester in 1895.

---

25 McKelvey, *Rochester on the Genesee*, 104.

---

26 www.landmarksociety.org/tours/index. Corn Hill Tour No. 17.

As Rochester's industrial development continued to grow, the city began taking on a definite cosmopolitan and sophisticated air. In 1875, there were three daily newspapers, which soon grew to five, and by 1884, the Democrat & Chronicle, which usually ran four pages, went as high as twelve. Amateur and professional theater productions were popular, offering serious drama, musicals and farce.[27] For outdoor entertainment, there was the Driving Park, located to the northwest of the intersection of today's Lake and Driving Park Avenues. Nothing compared with the throngs of 15,000 and more who gathered to see Grand Trotting Circuit races, circuses, bicycle races and national troupes such as Buffalo Bill's "Wild West Show." It was the center of a more free and open social life in Rochester.

Rochester Driving Park

An assortment of newcomers and former residents with new energies and fresh ideas transformed Rochester, in the latter half of the nineteenth century, from a city that specialized in handcrafted goods to one that embraced factory production. So began the labor movement. There were 735 industrial establishments in Rochester in 1880, more than double that of ten years earlier and by 1890 that number had more than doubled.[28] Many were small businesses–a third of these sold shoes and clothing, but larger businesses soon followed. Mortimer Reynolds, president of RSB from 1882 to 1892, guided the bank through these changing times.

---

27 McKelvey, *Rochester on the Genesee*, 120.

---

28 McKelvey, *Rochester on the Genesee*, 100.

Prominent Rochester ladies, most notably Susan B. Anthony, gave public expression to a growing Women's Rights movement. Retail stores expanded, especially the Boston Store on Main Street. It would later become the Sibley, Lindsay and Curr Company, the preeminent retail store in town for many years. Rochester's baseball team entered the International League in 1886, and remains the oldest team in the league and one of the longest-lasting continuous sport franchises in the U.S.

Frederick Cook was an RSB trustee for twenty-five years, from 1880 to 1905. A native of Germany, he moved to Rochester in 1852 and worked as a conductor on the Niagara Falls section of what would become the Buffalo, Rochester and Pittsburgh Railroad. His fluent German was an asset, since the travelers were primarily immigrants. During his twenty years with the railroad, he met and became close friends with George Pullman. When Pullman organized the Pullman Palace Car Company in 1867, Cook invested his savings in the stock, which became the foundation of his wealth. Cook was elected president of several Rochester concerns, including, in 1882, the Commercial Bank of Rochester, which later became the German-American Bank, and eventually, through various mergers and acquisitions, part of today's J. P. Morgan Chase Bank.[29]

In 1893, the U.S. suffered the worst depression since its founding, caused primarily by railroad overbuilding and shaky railroad financing. This set off a series of bank failures–some 500 in all–many in the West. Some Rochester businesses closed and many people lost their jobs, but "The Old Bank" was able to continue its prosperous ways. National unemployment ranged from 17 to 19 percent. The number of homeless children increased and the services of the "People's Rescue Mission" became more critical. The redoubtable Rochester Female Charitable Society, still very active since its debut in 1822, secured the financial backing to start an organization called the Door of Hope, a shelter for wayward girls expelled from stall saloons and other centers of vice.

Rufus Sibley became an RSB trustee in 1885. He came from Boston in 1868 and co-founded the Boston Store, which later became Rochester's leading retail establishment, the Sibley, Lindsay and Curr Company. Sibley was also a U of R trustee and became that university's board chair in 1895.

---

29 Peck, *History of Rochester*, 440, 443–44.

Rufus Sibley   *Hiram Watson Sibley*

Halbert S. Greenleaf, an RSB trustee from 1888 until 1906, was born in Vermont in 1827, and grew up on a farm. At age twenty-three he went to sea and served as a common sailor, before the mast. When Greenleaf enlisted as a private in the Union army, he was soon elected captain by his fellow soldiers. After his military service, he went to Shelburne Falls, Massachusetts and started a lock company. In 1867, he moved to Rochester and went into business with Joseph Sargent, who had invented a time lock. Banks now had their first reliable, burglar-proof safes. The Sargent & Greenleaf Company enjoyed much success and contributed greatly to Rochester's industrial growth. Greenleaf was later elected a member of the 48th and 52nd U.S. Congresses.

James Sibley Watson also joined RSB as a trustee in 1888. His father, Don Alonzo Watson, had partnered with Hiram Sibley in founding the forerunner of the Western Union Company in Rochester in 1851. James, at the age of seventeen, went West to take advantage of the Gold Rush in Wyoming and Nevada. A sportsman, he aided in the founding of the Genesee Valley Hunt Club, the Genesee Valley Club and the Country Club of Rochester. He and his wife contributed substantially to the establishment of the Memorial Art Gallery, and helped to found Rochester's Hochstein Music School in memory of their protégé, David Hochstein, a very talented violinist, who died in World War I. Watson was one of the founders of Security Trust Company, now part of Bank of America, and he served as its president from 1911 until 1940. He graduated from the U of R in 1881 without having attended a single class, choosing instead to take the examinations following study at home.

By 1900, Rochester's population had grown to 162,000, up from 130,000 ten years earlier, and the "City of Many Industries" had begun to metamorphose into "The Home of Quality Products." Hiram Watson Sibley, the son of Hiram Sibley, became an RSB trustee in 1892. He worked with his father, the co-founder of the Western Union Company, and his brother-in-law Hobart Atkinson (RSB trustee and future president). His business ventures included land development, railroads, and the seed business, as well as investing in timber and coal. After his father's death, he managed the affairs of the Sibley estate.

Albert Harris

Erickson Perkins (on right)

Other RSB trustees elected during this period were Albert Harris and Erickson Perkins. Albert Harris became a trustee in 1892. The Harris family's long involvement with the bank began in 1870 with his brother, Edward, who was both an RSB trustee and later the bank's attorney. Albert and his brother Edward were law partners. His sister, Elizabeth, married Harold P. Brewster, RSB president from 1909 to 1923. Albert became the senior vice president of the New York Central Railroad and chair of its executive committee. He was an intimate friend of New York Central president Chauncey Depew and the Vanderbilt family.

Erickson Perkins became an RSB trustee in 1895. His father, Gilman H. Perkins, had been an RSB trustee from 1875 to 1898. His home at 494 East Avenue has been the home of the American Association of University Women (AAUW) since 1947. His business, Erickson Perkins & Company, was a brokerage firm.

Thomas Finucane

Thomas Finucane was elected to the RSB board in 1899. From 1874 to 1880, he worked as a carpenter, and then joined the Hayden Company, a well-known custom furniture company. An incident there changed his life.[30] A prominent Rochester lady asked him to remodel her home, and upon his very successful completion of the project, Finucane launched his own company. Business took off and, in 1902, he expanded into contracting. Finucane built the first Kodak office building for George Eastman. He was an organizer, in 1892, of the Security Trust Company (now part of Bank of America), and also a director of the Lincoln Alliance (now J.P. Morgan Chase) and Union Trust (now HSBC) Banks. His son, B. Emmett Finucane, became a long-time president of Security Trust Company. Thomas Finucane built and lived in this home at 20 Portsmouth Terrace, still standing today.

Finucane Home

30 Lockwood Richard Doty, ed., *History of the Genesee Country* (Chicago: S. J. Clarke Publishing. Co., 1925), 3:134–37.

George Eastman   *A young George Eastman in Paris*

George Eastman was a trustee of RSB for twenty-eight years, from 1900 to
1928. Eastman was born in 1854 and his father died in 1862, leaving George,
his sisters Ellen and Emma, and his mother Maria Kilbourn Eastman,
almost penniless. Mrs. Eastman took in boarders to survive. George had to
quit school at the age of fourteen to help support the family. He worked for
$3 a week as a messenger boy for an insurance firm and studied accounting
at home in hopes of finding a better job. When he was twenty, he applied for
work at RSB. Board policy at the time required a vote on all new employees.

RSB
Trustees
Meeting
of 1911

The 1911 photo shown here of RSB trustees probably looks a lot like the
group that voted for George Eastman on April 8, 1874. The minutes of
that day indicate that on the third ballot he was elected a clerk, with a salary
of $700 per year, thus beginning a relationship of some sixty years with
"The Old Bank." One wonders what might have happened to Rochester and
photography had the vote gone differently.

Eastman soon worked his way up to junior bookkeeper at RSB. At that time, bookkeepers had to be audited every three years for security reasons, and in 1877 he was required by bank rules to take a vacation. When he told a fellow employee that he wanted to take his mandated vacation in Santo Domingo, his friend encouraged him to take pictures of the trip. Although the trip never materialized, the friend's suggestion altered the course of his life and history. Eastman knew nothing about photography then, but decided to study it. After lessons with two local photographers, he began to spend all of his leisure time on photography. He continued working at RSB until September 5, 1881, when the board accepted his resignation. While Eastman's stated reason for resigning was to pursue his interest in photography, his departure was actually precipitated by his belief that he had been passed over for a well-deserved promotion in favor of a trustee's relative. Today, neither the relative nor the trustee are known, but the incident led to Eastman's strong aversion to favoritism.[31] George Eastman had $3,000 in an RSB savings account when he left the bank. He said later that this was the original capital for the Eastman Dry Plate & Film Company, predecessor of the Eastman Kodak Company.[32]

Two Eastman personal RSB checks

Eastman's trustee book showing successor trustees including the author

A young man named Thomas Hawks became Eastman's replacement as junior bookkeeper at RSB. He was the grandfather of Thomas Harris Hawks who, in 1951, at age thirty-five, became RSB's president.

31 Elizabeth Brayer, *George Eastman: A Biography* (Baltimore: Johns Hopkins Press, 1996), 40.

32 Speare, *Rochester 100 Years Ago and Now*, 29.

Eastman's election to the RSB board in 1900 began a tradition of top Kodak executives serving as RSB trustees. These included CEOs William Vaughn, Louis Eilers, Walter Fallon, and Colby Chandler; executive vice president Donald McMaster; treasurers Marion Folsom and J. Donald Fewster; and Robert Murray, vice president and general comptroller. After RSB's merger in 1983 with Community Savings Bank, Michael Morley, Kodak's executive vice president and chief administrative officer, became an RCSB board member. Morley was also the chair of RIT's board of trustees from 2006 to 2009.

RSB trustee Hobart Atkinson became president of the bank in 1904 and served until 1908. The trustees elected during his tenure mark somewhat of a turning point in the provenance of trustees. In the earlier years, more than a few of RSB's trustees had been related in one way or another, through blood, business or marriage. While there may have been good reasons for this in Rochester's early days (because of the limited availability, size and quality of the "pool" of knowledgeable talent in the city), from this point forward, the trustees began to reach farther out to find their own replacements. Rochester's pool of talented businessmen had grown by leaps and bounds.

James G. Cutler

James G. Cutler was elected an RSB trustee in 1904. An architect, he and his brother were associates in controlling and operating Cutler Mail Chute patents. He was also a very popular Rochester mayor, from 1904 to 1905, and a U of R trustee.

William S. Morse

William S. Morse was an RSB trustee from 1905 until 1930. His family had been in the lumber business since 1842. The Morse Lumber Company, still operated by the Morse family, remains one of the oldest firms in Rochester. One of the secrets of its success may have been the location of its main office on West Main Street. The site, purchased from the Hollister Lumber Company, was the precise point where, early on, the east/west Erie Canal, the north/south Genesee Valley Canal, and the Buffalo, Rochester and Pittsburgh Railroad all unloaded their lumber cargo, right at the front door of Morse Lumber. Morse's death in 1930 severed an important link with the city's romantic past. He and his father had made significant contributions to Rochester's development, not only in a material way, but as public, spirited citizens, willing and able to assume leadership in civic enterprises. Morse's older brother, Charles C., was also an RSB trustee, from 1871 until 1897.

CHAPTER FIVE

ROCHESTER'S
GOLDEN ERA

Harold P. Brewster, trustee from 1899 to 1925, was also RSB president for
fourteen years, from 1909 to 1923. The period of his affiliation with RSB,
the first quarter of the twentieth century, was a great era in Rochester.
New industries were booming and everything was pretty much "right with
the world." By 1920, the population had swelled to 295,000, from 162,000
in 1900. This was in the aftermath of what was known as the Bankers
Panic of 1907, during which the New York Stock Exchange fell 50 percent.
The primary cause of this panic was that many New York City banks restricted
market liquidity, resulting in an extreme loss of depositor confidence.
Another problem was the notable lack of a statutory lender of last resort,
a void that J. P. Morgan valiantly tried to fill, only somewhat successfully.

The result was the creation of the Federal Reserve System in 1913, which, in
effect, became the central bank and lender of last resort. Nationally chartered
banks were required to join the system, and state banks had the option of
doing so. The Federal Reserve established a more orderly method of managing
the nation's money supply. Consequently, banks operated in a stronger
financial climate and the public's confidence in the banking system grew.
The value of this is clearly seen in the financial climate of 2008–2009.
Without the liquidity afforded by the Federal Reserve System, there would
have been no way to counteract the financial crisis. This liquidity was
available in the Great Depression years of the 1930s, but was not utilized,
which perhaps contributed to the length of that Depression.

33 Gilman Perkins (grand nephew of John Craig Powers)
    "Be There, You'll Never Forget It," paper presented to
    the Humdrum and Oasis Clubs, c. 2006.

Harold P. Brewster   *John Craig Powers*

John Craig Powers joined the RSB board in 1906 and served for forty-nine years, until 1955. He was the son of Daniel Powers, who had built the Powers Building and the Powers Hotel, and started the Powers Bank in 1850, using RSB trustees Everard Peck and Isaac Hills as character references to the public. Craig Powers, as he was known, was the stroke on the Harvard crew in 1892, which beat Yale by eleven lengths. After graduation, still elated with the victory over the university's arch rival, Craig had visions of a European fling. To his dismay, his taskmaster father sent him a telegram telling him that on July 7th he was to report for duty at the bank. Craig reportedly told his father, "That's my birthday." Dan's response was, "You won't forget to be here then, will you?"[33] Craig Powers went on to run the Powers Bank for many years. In 1919, it merged into the newly-created Lincoln Alliance Bank Group that ultimately became part of today's J. P. Morgan Chase Bank.

The Powers Building

Good things continued to happen in Rochester, such as the formation of a local Boy Scout Council, which started at the YMCA in 1910. In 1915, Howard Barrows, head of Rochester's Board of Education, asked RSB to create a School Savings Department, which ultimately became a great success. Here's how it worked: school children could deposit any amount–five cents or more–and a passbook was issued to them when their account totaled one dollar. This practice was meant to instill a lifetime habit of saving, and create positive banking relationships. Rumor has it that the practice continued until some time in the 1950s, when teachers' unions bargained away their obligation to collect this money. As late as the mid-1970s, RSB was the only Rochester bank that offered children a passbook account, a legacy of the "School Savings" days.

School Savings Stamps

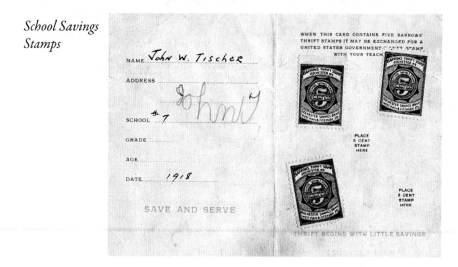

School Savings Deposit Slip

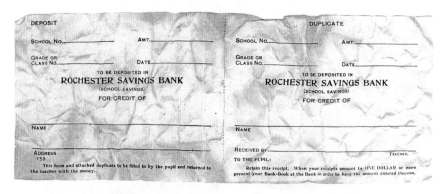

Edward Harris Jr.   *Daniel M. Beach*

Edward Harris Jr., a 1900 graduate of Cornell Law School, was elected to
the RSB board in 1911. Harris became a senior partner in the Harris, Haven,
Beach & Harris law firm, the successor to the law firm started by his brother,
Albert, and father, Edward. He served as the RSB bank attorney for
thirty-seven years, from 1911 to 1948. His wife, Mary Peck, was a descendant
of RSB founding trustee Everard Peck, and his sister Elizabeth married
Harold P. Brewster, RSB president and trustee. Harris was also a U of R trustee.

Harris' business partner, Daniel M. Beach, became an RSB trustee in 1912.
Fifteen years earlier, Beach had joined the Harris & Harris law firm,[34] becoming
a partner in 1905. Harris, Haven, Beach & Harris was the forerunner of today's
Harris Beach PLLC, with its two hundred attorneys located in nine offices.

William Drescher served on the RSB board from 1908 until 1936. Born in
Germany, he came to the U.S. in 1873 to join Bausch & Lomb in New York City.
In 1888, he was transferred to the company's Rochester headquarters, where he
met Ann Bausch, the daughter of co-founder John Jacob Bausch, and married
her two years later. Eventually, Drescher became treasurer of Bausch & Lomb
and had financial interests in many Rochester enterprises.

During World War I, trustee George Eastman purchased $2.5 million
worth of Liberty Bonds. RSB also bought Liberty Bonds, and resold them,
in increments with weekly installments, to small subscribers. Over 110,000
individuals availed themselves of this opportunity. This has been described
as the first payroll savings plan in America, and RSB provided free safekeeping
for the bonds.

---

34 Peck, *History of Rochester*, 729.

M. Herbert Eisenhart

Walter L. Todd

M. Herbert Eisenhart was an RSB trustee for thirty-seven years, starting in 1924. Grandson-in-law of John Jacob Bausch, the co-founder of Bausch & Lomb, he was also a long-time CEO of Bausch & Lomb. Eisenhart served as an RIT trustee for more than fifty years, thus upholding the historical ties between RIT and the founders of Bausch & Lomb. Eisenhart was also a U of R trustee.

Walter L. Todd was elected to RSB's board of trustees in 1924. A Cornell graduate (1909) and trustee, he was president of his family's business, the Todd Company, makers of the first check "Protectograph," among other banking products. In 1933, the company made emergency scrip (a temporary substitute for cash) for Rochester when FDR's "bank holiday" temporarily closed all the banks in the nation. (This is further explained in Chapter 6). The Todd Company became part of the Burroughs Corporation in 1955. He and Eisenhart were the earliest trustees still active on the RSB board when I joined it in 1960.

Edwin Allen Stebbins joined the RSB board in 1923. He had come to Rochester in 1888 when his father was asked to be the minister at Central Presbyterian Church. A graduate of Andover and Yale, he was a member of Skull & Bones, Yale's secret society of select seniors. On the death of RSB President Henry Hanford in 1927, Stebbins became RSB's president, serving from 1927 until 1951. He was highly respected and known as the "Chief" to family and bank employees. His term of office spanned an extraordinary period of growth and great turbulence in Rochester. Stebbins was also chair of the YMCA from 1910 to 1916.

Edwin Allen Stebbins   *40 Franklin Street*

In the summer of 1943, Rochester Savings Bank hired me as a bank messenger. This was only finalized, however, after I had been summoned to Mr. Stebbins's office and gotten his approval. My weekly pay was $16.50, which included a half day of work on Saturdays. One of my duties was to carry money between the bank's two branches in a police motorcycle sidecar. I enjoyed riding up Main Street with the officer and, from time to time, I raised my hands together to create the appearance of being manacled. (This gesturing stopped when a family friend saw me). The whole operation ended one day when Mr. Stebbins observed me leaving with a bag of money, alone.

In 1927, the bank's first branch opened at 40 Franklin Street. Considered one of the finest Byzantine banking floors in the country, the interior of this building features a stunning wall mural by Ezra Winter, who also contributed work to Rochester's Eastman Theater. George Eastman's hand can clearly be seen in the Franklin Street building, which was designed by McKim, Mead and White, who also designed George Eastman's house. It is listed on the National Register of Historic Places.

Inside
40 Franklin Street

Ezra Winter mural
(on right)

F. Harper Sibley   *Albert A. Hopeman*

F. Harper Sibley was elected an RSB trustee in 1927. Just eight years later, in 1935, he became president of the U.S. Chamber of Commerce. In 1945, acting as a consultant for the chamber, Sibley participated in a modest way in the forming of the United Nations.[35] He succeeded his father, RSB trustee Hiram Watson Sibley, in managing the family businesses. A Harvard graduate and non-practicing attorney, F. Harper enjoyed private financial success and maintained the Sibley family tradition of community involvement. He chaired the YMCA board twice, from 1920 to 1926, and again from 1931 to 1939.

Albert A. Hopeman had a close relationship with George Eastman and filled his seat on the RSB board in 1929. I, in turn, took the Eastman/Hopeman seat when I joined RSB in 1960. Hopeman headed the A.W. Hopeman & Sons Company, the general contracting firm that built the Eastman Theater, Eastman School of Music, and Kodak's main office tower. The firm was also general contractor for the eleven original buildings at the U of R's River Campus. The Hopeman family gave the U of R both its original library chime, in 1930, and the Hopeman Engineering Laboratory. Hopeman's firm built a spectacular RSB Board of Trustees table, at cost, when no other contractor could be found. The myopic state banking department seriously questioned this "doing business with a trustee."

---

35 McKelvey, *Rochester on the Genesee*, 208.

CHAPTER SIX

THE DEPRESSION YEARS
AND
WORLD WAR II

In 1929, the Rochester Savings Bank had 100,000 customers, $57 million in deposits, and $9 million in reserves. Despite the stock market crash, not only did "The Old Bank" and all other New York State savings banks survive the Depression, but they also managed to pay their depositors interest as usual. Once again in troubled times, RSB provided financial security for Rochesterians. In large measure, this stability was due to the bank's investments in home mortgages and U.S. government securities. RSB had also invested in the highest grade municipal, railroad, and public utility bonds, of a nature readily convertible into cash. In July 1931, the city of Rochester boasted 42 percent home ownership–the highest rate in the country![36]

RSB developed a flexible system of repaying mortgage loans that enabled many who would have lost their homes to keep them. The bank worked closely with hard-pressed mortgagors to avoid foreclosure if at all possible. Among the techniques developed at this time was the "interest added to principal" monthly payment schedule. Previously, traditional monthly mortgage payments were "principal only," with mortgage interest paid in lump sums once or twice a year. The revised RSB system combined principal and interest in each monthly mortgage payment. Eventually all mortgage contracts were drawn up in this way.

---

36   Turri, *Rochester Savings Bank*, 61.

The national financial system suffered a total collapse in early 1933. On Sunday, March 5, 1933, newly-elected President Franklin Roosevelt declared a mandatory bank holiday, closing all banks in order to determine which ones were solvent. The Rochester banks decided to issue their own scrip to keep the community afloat. On Monday, March 6, 1933, the Todd Company had an order for four million new notes, two million of which were issued. When the Rochester banks reopened on March 14, the two million notes were redeemed, except for a few which are still privately held by collectors. The banks had been strong enough to force the city administration to accept their fiscal leadership; which contrasted sharply with many other cities where the banks became insolvent.

Trustees elected during this turbulent era reflected the changing times; their affiliations were often on a national scale. Marion B. Folsom, who became an RSB trustee in 1931, was among those who served on many levels. After growing up in Georgia, he earned a Harvard MBA in 1914, and was hired at Eastman Kodak the same year. Folsom designed Kodak's corporate pension plan, which went into effect on January 1, 1929. President Roosevelt summoned him to Washington, D.C. in 1934 to help create the national Social Security plan, and he also served as a director of the Federal Reserve Bank of New York. Folsom was the treasurer of Eastman Kodak from 1935 to 1953, when President Eisenhower named him Undersecretary of the Treasury. Two years later he became the U.S. Secretary of Health, Education, and Welfare.

Marion Folsom

At age 33, I was awed to be on the same board with Marion Folsom, a strong contributor at board meetings. I recall the unmistakable, low, Southern tone of his voice, and that his comments frequently included, "Now, when I was down in Washington..." Several of the other RSB board members who were a bit hard of hearing would often say, "I wish you'd speak up, Marion."

Thomas G. Spencer   *Richard M. Harris*

Another Harvard graduate, Thomas G. Spencer was an RSB trustee from 1933 until 1961. His wife, Harriet Hollister, was the daughter of earlier RSB Trustee Granger Hollister, whose grandfather had founded Rochester's Hollister Lumber Company in 1832. Spencer was president of Hollister Lumber for many years. His family residence is still standing at 1005 East Avenue, a home which had been built by RSB bank attorney Edward Harris in 1867. A gentleman of the old school, Spencer was treated with great deference by RSB board members. Somewhat hard of hearing, he occupied the place of honor at the board table, on President Tom Hawks' left. One of his proudest accomplishments was a gift to New York State of 679 acres, south of Honeoye Lake, now known as the Harriet Hollister Spencer Memorial State Recreation Area.

Richard M. Harris was an RSB trustee from 1933 until 1962. A Princeton graduate, he was CEO of the Alling & Cory Paper Company, a long-time Rochester business which was located on the site of today's Frontier Field. Harris was also president of the National Paper Trade Association and a director of Lincoln Rochester Bank (later J.P. Morgan Chase). He served as YMCA board chair from 1946 to 1948.

Stebbins Dinner for RSB Trustees and Officers, 1950.

James P. B. Duffy was elected to the RSB board in 1933 and served for twenty-seven years. A Harvard Law School graduate, he was elected to the U.S. Congress for one term, from 1935 to 1937. Upon leaving Congress, Governor Lehman appointed him a New York State Supreme Court judge. He later returned to the practice of law, but was always referred to as "Judge." As the oldest RSB trustee, he had the privilege of toasting Marion Hawks as she retired from the cocktail hour preceding the annual all-male, black-tie trustee dinners during Tom Hawks' years as president. This followed the protocol set by his predecessor, Edwin Allen Stebbins.

James P.B. Duffy

Mercer Brugler became an RSB trustee in 1937. A U of R graduate, he was a member of Phi Beta Kappa. He joined the Pfaudler Company in 1926, and worked his way up to CEO in 1959. In 1968, Pfaudler became part of the new Sybron Corporation, and Brugler became Sybron's CEO. He was U of R board chair for three years and chair of its executive committee for seven years. Brugler was a lifetime U of R trustee, and YMCA board chair from 1952 to 1954.

Mercer Brugler   *Ernest Paviour*

Ernest Paviour, another U of R graduate, served on the RSB board for eighteen years, from 1940 to 1958. After gaining extensive newspaper experience with the Gannett Company, he joined his father's insurance brokerage firm. Paviour was a public relations confidant of George Eastman, who often asked Paviour for his opinion on Eastman's ideas for improving Rochester. There were times when Paviour would float "trial balloons" in the community for Mr. Eastman on these ideas. Paviour chaired the YMCA board from 1939 until 1940.

Stebbins Dinner Gold Plate Table Setting

Donald W. Gilbert

Donald W. Gilbert was an RSB trustee for nine years, from 1948 to 1957, the first board member who came from a strictly academic field. Having earned a Ph.D. in Economics from Harvard, he became the U of R provost. Gilbert played a role in many civic organizations, including the Bureau of Municipal Research, the Council of Postwar Problems for Rochester & Monroe County, the Economic Advisory Committee to the State Legislative Committee on Interstate Cooperation, and the Brookhaven National Laboratory.

During the World War II years, Rochester boomed. RSB's hours were changed to accommodate war workers, many of whom purchased the 572,000 U.S. War Bonds sold by the bank for $27.5 million. RSB bought $77.9 million in bonds for its own account. The post-war VA (Veteran Administration) mortgages for returning servicemen, contracted mainly between 1945 and 1955, helped RSB's portfolio jump from $24.8 million to $107.4 million. Under the G.I. Bill of Rights, veterans were entitled to mortgages with low interest rates, and many took advantage of them, often with mortgages of thirty years in duration. This would hurt the bank within a decade or so, as competition and interest rates heated up. But the bank remained heavily committed to these long-term, low-yielding assets. At the same time, deposits also grew dramatically, increasing from $58 million in 1945 to $150 million in 1955.

Industries began to change, reflecting the national integration of the economy. Many Rochester companies became affiliated with larger national firms, and Rochester and Monroe County began to reflect the nationwide move to the suburbs. Another extreme growth surge occurred in academics. Because the G.I. bill also paid for a veteran's advanced education, a quarter of a million of them entered college.

CHAPTER SEVEN

THE WAR ENDS
BUT
TROUBLE LOOMS

Joseph C. Wilson, a U of R graduate, was elected to RSB's board of trustees in 1948. Wilson's Haloid Company sold photographic paper. The same year he joined RSB's board, Wilson gambled his family business's future and made a deal with Chester Carlson, a patent lawyer who had invented a xerographic process. Ultimately, their association evolved into the Xerox Corporation, which emerged as one of the most stunning business success stories of the last century, creating enormous wealth for the community. As CEO of Xerox from 1961 to 1967, Wilson took the organization to historic heights. He also chaired the U of R board from 1959 to 1967. The university unequivocally maintains that Joe Wilson and George Eastman were the chief architects of the successful direction taken by the U of R in the twentieth century.[37]

Joseph C. Wilson

---

37 *Rochester Review*, University of Rochester Alumni Gazette 67
    No. 2 (Winter 2004–2005), University of Rochester.

The Wilson and Carlson families became generous philanthropists in the Rochester community. Among the many Xerox-related contributions to the area are the Chester Carlson Center for Imaging Science at RIT, the Carlson Library at U of R, and the Carlson MetroCenter YMCA. The Wilson family created the Joseph C. Wilson Health Center, and the Marie C. and Joseph C. Wilson Foundation, which supports housing, health instruction, education, social services, and the arts.[38] In addition, the two most generous U of R donors were George Eastman and Joseph Wilson until the University received a $30 million gift in October of 2008. However, considering the current value of money relative to the dollar value at the time it was given, George Eastman remains the U of R's largest benefactor.

Personally, I was awed by Joe Wilson. He was a great man, a great leader, and, I think, a true genius, who was also unfailingly kind, unfailingly quick, and low key. He had clear vision and a modest, down-to-earth approach. It is safe to say that he and George Eastman had as great an effect on the city of Rochester as any other men in its history. RSB was indeed fortunate to have had both as trustees. After Wilson, several other top Xerox executives were elected to the RSB board, including CEOs C. Peter McColough and David Kearns, and board chair Sol Linowitz.

Donald McMaster was elected to the RSB board in 1949. A Cornell graduate, he rose in the Eastman Kodak Company to the positions of executive vice president, director, and chair of the executive committee. He effectively ran Kodak during World War II when CEO Thomas J. Hargrave was in Washington helping with the war effort. (Hargrave and other top national executives were known as "$1.00 a year men" because that's what they were paid for their efforts). McMaster was especially kind to me as a young trustee.

Edward Harris Jr. (son and grandson of the bank attorneys who shared his name) was elected to the RSB board in 1949. Continuing the long Harris law firm relationship with RSB, he was the third Harris to serve as the bank's attorney, from 1960 to 1983. A graduate of Princeton and then Cornell Law School, he was also a cousin of Thomas Harris Hawks, RSB president from 1951 to 1970. A champion rower and an avid horseman, fox hunter, and carriage driver, he helped found Morven Park Equestrian Institute in Leesburg, Virginia, dedicated to equestrian education and instructor development. He was also YMCA board chair from 1958 to 1960.

---

38 Marie C. and Joseph C. Wilson Foundation Website
    "Foundation Information,"
    http://www.mcjcwilsonfoundation.org/foundation.cfm.

Donald McMaster *Edward Harris, Jr.*

Thomas Harris Hawks was 33 years old when he was elected an RSB trustee in 1949. A Cornell graduate with a Harvard MBA, he became RSB's president two years later. Hawks added the title of chairman in 1955 and carried both titles until 1970. A man of immense integrity, he was one of the giants of the community and accepted a myriad of civic responsibilities, which he regarded as a sacred trust. The community boards on which he served represented Rochester's backbone. During Hawks' tenure, race problems arose in Rochester. Seeds of racial discord had been sown as migrants moved to Rochester from the South, and, in response, city residents moved to the suburbs. In 1964, race riots left deep wounds. Hawks played a leading role in creating Rochester Jobs, Inc., widely regarded as the most successful response to the demands of the local African-American community's grassroots civil rights organization, FIGHT (Freedom-Integration-God-Honor-Today). Hawks remained deeply involved in almost all key areas of the community, and helped steer both RSB and the city through some very painful times. In the great tradition of their predecessors, Hawks and the other trustees consistently drew the bank and its home neighborhood closer together.

Thomas Harris Hawks

As a modest example of his integrity, Tom Hawks supplied cigars at board meetings for those trustees who enjoyed them. He paid for them himself, not considering it to be a proper bank expense.

The city's population grew from 295,000 in 1920, to 332,000 by 1950, when the population of Greater Rochester reached one million.
At this time, the flight to the suburbs was on–Rochester had become a metropolis. Business mergers were everywhere–locally and with national companies. Hawks saw this as an indication of Rochester's technological vitality and not as a threat to local autonomy. A new RSB building was built at the corner of Main and Fitzhugh to replace the classic building that had stood there for 100 years. It had the first drive-up auto teller facility in the city.

New bank

*Drive-up
teller window*

By the late 1960s, banks were becoming increasingly competitive. During the Great Depression of the 1930s, the Federal Reserve System had implemented Regulation Q, which, among other things, capped the interest rates that commercial banks could offer on savings accounts, and did not allow them to pay interest on checking accounts. Savings banks were permitted to pay higher interest rates on savings accounts than commercial banks. In 1970, Regulation Q was amended and the interest rate differential between commercial and savings banks was cut in half. Further erosion continued to occur, and the year 1980 saw the start of a final phase-out of the differential, which ended completely in 1986. But in the meantime, during the 1970s, large institutional deposits had began to migrate to Europe where interest rates were not limited by Regulation Q. Money market funds pooled cash to invest in money market instruments. Competition for savings accounts also increased with the advent of brokerage houses and other unregulated non-banking institutions. All of these competitive factors caused a dramatic and precarious increase in interest rates.

In 1959, 94% of RSB's assets were income producing. They fell into three main categories: 78 percent were invested in mortgages (mostly long-term); 13 percent were in bonds; and 3 percent were in newly-permitted, preferred stocks that were well-selected and high-grade or were invested in New York State's newly-created Institutional Investors Mutual Fund (IIMF). These investments all had low fixed yields, which caused problems with the onset of "disintermediation"–the deposit runoff triggered by commercial banks and non-commercial sources (such as brokerage houses), which were increasingly competing for deposits. Savings banks could not move their low-yielding assets into high-yielding ones because most of them were tied up in long-term mortgages, and the rest were in safe but low-yielding securities. As marketplace interest rates went up rapidly, savings banks couldn't follow without being forced to spend capital.

During the two decades that spanned the Hawks presidency, several notable trustees were elected to the board, Sol Linowitz, Arthur L. Stern, and Lucius (Bob) Gordon.

Sol Linowitz

Sol Linowitz joined the RSB board in 1955. As a partner in the Harris Beach law firm, he was chief counsel for one of its clients, Xerox Corporation. He became Xerox chairman of the board (but never CEO), and also chaired its executive committee from 1961 to 1966. He left Rochester in 1965, settling in Washington, D.C., and was soon immersed in governmental matters. President Lyndon Johnson appointed him Ambassador to the Organization of American States (OAS) in 1966. However, when Richard Nixon took office, Linowitz quickly resigned his ambassadorship because he had no desire to be part of the Nixon administration. He played key roles in the Middle East peace negotiations and the Panama Canal Treaty under President Jimmy Carter.

In the late 1960s, RSB president Tom Hawks became president of the New York State Association of Savings Banks. At that time it was customary and considered proper to hold the association's annual meetings at somewhat exotic locations. Tom scheduled one of these meetings in San Juan, Puerto Rico, and asked Sol Linowitz, ambassador to the OAS, to be the principal speaker. My wife and I were invited to the meeting and Tom let it be known that we were to be sure that Sol and his wife were "properly taken care of." Life was rather sweet for us in our suite next to the Linowitz's, on the top floor of the Caribe Hilton in San Juan! While there, Sol told me that his election to the RSB board had been one of the key moments in his career.

---

39   Stacy A. Cordery, *Alice: Alice Roosevelt Longworth,
     from White House Princess to Washington Power Broker.*
     (New York: Penguin, 2007), 455.

Arthur L. Stern

Sol also attracted the interest of longtime Washington doyenne, Alice Roosevelt Longworth, and he was a frequent guest in her salon and at her poker table.[39] In 1998, President Clinton awarded Linowitz the highest civilian honor in the U.S., the Presidential Medal of Freedom. Recipients are chosen based on the individual's especially meritorious contributions to the security or national interests of our country, to world peace, to cultural life, or to some other significant public or private endeavor. President Carter said that Linowitz "was a dedicated public servant with great political courage, an encyclopedic knowledge of foreign affairs and unexcelled diplomatic skills."[40] Sol Linowitz was 91 when he died on March 18, 2005. The only other trustees to have played major roles on the national stage were Marion Folsom and David Kearns.

Arthur L. Stern, elected an RSB trustee in 1955, graduated from Yale and then Harvard Law School. He was a partner in what is today Rochester's Nixon Peabody law firm. He continued the strong RSB connection with RIT by serving as an RIT trustee from 1950 until his death. He chaired its board from 1961 to 1976, and effectively served RIT for a third of a century. He also helped decide, build and move RIT out of downtown Rochester to its new campus in Henrietta. Additionally, he helped establish The National Technical Institute for the Deaf at RIT. The Stern Board Room is named in his honor. [41]

---

40 Obituary. *Democrat and Chronicle*, March 19, 2005, 19A.

---

41 Rochester Institute of Technology, Board of Trustees Resolution (honoring Arthur L. Stern), July 10, 1987, RIT Archives.

Lucius R. Gordon   *William Vaughn*

Lucius R. (Bob) Gordon joined RSB's board in 1955. A graduate of Andover and Yale, he received an honorary doctorate from RIT. The same year he joined RSB, he became an RIT trustee and served as its board vice chair for a number of years. He was the major contributor to RIT's $25 million Gordon Field House, which was named in his honor. It is second in size only to the Blue Cross Arena as a Rochester public facility.

William Vaughn, elected an RSB trustee in 1959, was a Rhodes Scholar. A graduate of Vanderbilt University and the U of R, he "grew up" at Kodak, becoming the last CEO (from 1960 to 1970) to have personally known George Eastman. Vaughn had a "grandfatherly" manner that stood him in good stead in dealing with the racial challenges of the 1960s, which involved Kodak directly–and quite harshly. He handled difficult events with great forbearance.

As a director of the YMCA, he played a key role in making it possible for that organization to accept a large contribution from a local brewery. Over the years, the Y had been a "teetotalling" institution, and whether to take such a gift became a matter for the board to decide. Vaughn paved the way for acceptance by saying, "I think the devil has had the money long enough." Another popular story about Vaughn, who eschewed using Kodak's corporate airplane for non-Kodak matters, occurred on a commercial flight back to Rochester from a Vanderbilt University trustee's meeting in Nashville, Tennessee. Vaughn was chair of his alma mater's board of trustees at the time. As he moved down the aisle to his coach seat, he said hello to a number of Kodak employees who were returning from a sales conference– they were seated in first class! He was also a "dollar-a-year" man in Washington, D.C. during World War II.

John H. Castle   *Louis A. Langie*

The late 1950s and 1960s brought a number of new trustees to the board, including Louis A. Langie, Ernest J. Howe, John H. Castle and a former bank messenger, me.

John H. ("Jack") Castle joined the RSB board in 1959. He attended Andover and Yale, where he was a great football tackle. Castle headed the Wilmot Castle Company, makers of sterilizers and operating room lights, that later became part of Sybron Corporation. When Tom Hawks first asked the RSB board to consider electing a woman as trustee, Jack, a big playful man, broke the huge silence that greeted Tom's remarks by saying that, if that happened, he would be "unable to properly express himself at meetings." It was a few more years before a woman appeared in the boardroom.

Louis A. Langie was elected in 1960. He was the head of Langie Fuel Service, Inc., a company started by his grandfather in 1872. Among the many community activities which he supported, Langie chaired the Boy Scouts, the Chamber of Commerce and the United Way. Georgetown University honored him with its highest alumni award.

A 1949 graduate of Yale, I joined the board in 1960. The Rochester insurance brokerage firm where I was a partner was eventually merged into the international firm Marsh & McClennan. At Yale I was a baseball teammate of future U.S. president George Herbert Walker Bush and competed in the first two NCAA College World Series ever played. I chaired the YMCA board from 1975–1977.

James C. Duffus   *Ernest J. Howe*

When Tom Hawks asked me to join the board, I was flabbergasted. Later, I learned that I replaced him as the youngest trustee ever elected, I still can't figure out why I was chosen, but what a ride! At the time, I needed to move my family to a larger home because our newly-born third child's "room" was a walk-in closet. Trustee fees had become legal several decades earlier and they gave me the ability to buy the house we had chosen. The custom of the day permitted a sister savings bank to give me a mortgage at a discounted rate–a practice unheard of today. Tom Hawks mentored me and I was most fortunate because he was the model of a great citizen/businessman.

Ernest J. Howe became an RSB board member in 1961. He was president of the Rochester Gas & Electric Corporation. A financial advisor to the FHA in the 1930s, he was also the chief financial advisor to the Temporary National Economic Committee of the U.S. Senate in 1938 and 1939. Howe had an encyclopedic investment expertise, especially in bonds.

C. Peter McColough was elected to the board in 1962. His career at Xerox began in 1954 at the age of 31, and he became the company's president and CEO serving from 1968 to 1982. Early in his tenure, he moved the Xerox headquarters from Rochester to Connecticut. At the time, there was a great deal of furor over his decision. The stated reason for the move was to obtain easier access to the financial markets of New York City, but there was speculation that it was really caused by a desire to get Xerox out from under the huge shadow cast in Rochester by Eastman Kodak Company. Xerox founder Joseph Wilson was believed to have approved the move reluctantly, recognizing the fact that McColough now was the CEO.

C. Peter McColough　　　　　　　　*F. Allen Macomber*

F. Allen Macomber became an RSB trustee in 1963. An architect, his firm designed the "new" East High School on East Main Street, and the Greece Olympia and Arcadia High Schools, all of which were considered break-through designs of the day. His knowledge of architecture proved very helpful in handling many commercial mortgage investments.

J. Donald Fewster joined the RSB board in 1964. The treasurer of Eastman Kodak Company, he was also CEO of Eastman Savings and Loan (currently known as ESL Federal Credit Union and no longer associated with Kodak).

Elected to the RSB board in 1965, Dr. Alice Foley was not only the first woman RSB trustee, but also the first woman bank trustee in Rochester. A magna cum laude graduate of Nazareth College in 1930, Foley became the college's president in 1972. Prior to this, she was a teacher and administrator in the Brighton (NY) public school system, and was elected twice as president of the New York State Teacher's Association.

J. Donald Fewster　　　　　　　　*Alice Foley*

Bruce B. Bates   *William G. von Berg*

Bruce B. Bates, elected an RSB trustee in 1965, is a senior vice president of the Morgan Stanley Smith Barney brokerage firm. A Yale graduate, he also holds a masters degree from MIT. Bates was RIT's board chair from 1984 to 1987. A strong contributor to many community non-profit boards, he played a particularly effective role in the merger of RSB and Community Savings Bank. He follows in the tradition of great Rochester citizens.

William von Berg was also elected a trustee in 1965. At the time, he was the financial vice president of Sybron Corporation, and became its CEO in 1975. With his strong accounting background, he offered key insights into the bank's financial reports.

Dr. Louis Eilers also came to the RSB board in 1965. The son of an Illinois grocer, he started at Kodak in 1934 and became president in 1967, CEO in 1969, and chairman of the board in 1970. Eilers shared with William Vaughn the challenge of dealing with the race problems of the day. Eilers struck me as brilliant, but I felt he could be a very tough taskmaster.

Dr. Louis K. Eilers   *William E. Lee*

Robert B. Frame   *Andrew D. Wolfe*

Robert B. (Bud) Frame became an RSB trustee in 1968. He was executive vice president of Case-Hoyt, Inc., a fine commercial printer in Rochester. When that company was sold, he acquired Forbes Products, Inc., a firm that produced advertising materials. After selling Forbes Products, he helped create Trillium Associates, a venture capital private equity company.

Elected an RSB trustee in 1968, Andrew D. (Andy) Wolfe was a brilliant writer who cared deeply about the history of Rochester and its suburbs. Wolfe was the publisher of many area newspapers, including the Brighton-Pittsford Post and the New York-Pennsylvania Collector. He and his wife Vivienne restored Richardson's Tavern in Bushnell's Basin to the glory it had enjoyed in the Erie Canal days. He also started the Pittsford Historical Society.

William E. Lee joined the board in 1969. A Harvard graduate, Bill Lee spent forty-five years in the retail department store business. For fifteen years he was president of the venerable Sibley, Lindsay & Curr Company, started in 1868 by RSB Trustee Rufus Sibley. No one cared more about his customers than Bill Lee, who referred to them as his "precious customers." He'd do anything for them. Once he decided to honor the store's biggest customer by creating a public relations event around an award to be presented to that person. It didn't work out so well, however, because it turned out that the store's biggest customer was his wife, Joyce.

CHAPTER EIGHT

TROUBLE
ARRIVES

As discussed earlier, some federal banking regulations which had been in effect since the Depression, were changed in the 1970s. The competition of commercial banks with savings banks increased dramatically. At the same time, non-banking, non-regulated organizations such as brokerage houses appeared on the scene. They were able to offer many of the same services at better rates. The next two trustees were instrumental in managing "The Old Bank" during this difficult period.

F. Stanley DeVoy was elected RSB trustee and president in 1970. In 1928, the RSB had hired twenty-year old DeVoy as a clearing house clerk. For the next forty-two years he served the bank in almost every capacity. His personal history was a living testimony to the dedication which guided RSB through its 152 years of prosperity.[42] He and Henry Hanford were the only two career employees of RSB to become trustees and also presidents.

Frederick G. Ray joined the RSB board in 1971 as the only trustee elected during DeVoy's tenure. Ray came to Rochester from his presidency of the Village Savings Bank in Port Chester, New York. He was simultaneously elected president of RSB and added the title of chairman in 1974. Like most RSB trustees, Ray was civic-minded and active in the community. A trustee of RIT, he also headed the Boy Scout Council, and was involved with the Rotary Club, receiving its highest award.

---

42 Turri, *Rochester Savings Bank*, 87.

F. Stanley DeVoy

Frederick G. Ray

Ray and DeVoy led the bank during the perilous years when virtually all savings banks in the country saw their prosperity disappear in a downward spiral. Savings banks had to pay higher interest rates to keep their depositors, but were hindered by the albatross of long-term, low-yielding mortgages. In the late 1970s, savings banks had an average of 66 percent of their assets locked into mortgages, compared to commercial banks, with only 14 percent of their assets in mortgages. Traditionally, savings banks invested in long-term, government-backed securities with modest yields. In 1979, this figure had shriveled sharply, to $123 million. Revenues continued to plummet, and in 1981, the losses were an astounding $1.7 billion. This resulted in a rapid invasion of the capital reserves that had accumulated over many years.

RSB's profit of $3.10 million in 1978 was followed, three and a half years later, in the first half of 1982, by a loss of $34 million. The bank's surplus-to-assets ratio fell from 6.5 percent in 1978, to 4.1 percent in the first half of 1982. There was no end in sight. RSB's six month loss of $34 million in the first half of 1982 was more than tripled by Community Savings Bank, which lost $11.9 million in that same period. Nationally, during the first three years of the 1980s, mutual savings banks sustained operating losses of nearly $3.3 billion, the equivalent of more than 28 percent of the industry's reserves at year end 1980. A merger became inevitable if Rochester Savings Bank and Community Savings Bank were to survive. They merged on July 1, 1983, and the $15 million deficit they sustained that year was an amazing improvement over their combined losses of $32 million in 1982.

Walter A. Fallon   *Dr. Francena Miller*

However, this union only bought time. What saved the day was the 1986
conversion of the bank into a stock institution. The only other savings
bank in Rochester at that time, Monroe Savings Bank, failed on January
26, 1990 – along with fifty-seven other savings banks nationwide. Most of
the savings banks (and savings and loan institutions) that did not fail were
either acquired or had to merge. The handwriting was on the wall. Mammoth
financial institutions had formed across the country, and their ability to
compete was overwhelming. The extraordinary era of the savings bank was
coming to a close.

Fred Ray was the last president of the RSB. A number of trustees were elected
during his final years, including two more women. Walter A. Fallon became a
board member in 1972. A graduate of Union College, he joined Kodak in 1941
and rose to become its CEO from 1970 to 1982. If memory serves me correctly,
he was the first trustee to suggest that RSB needed to seek a new direction.
He said this at a board meeting during the late 1970s, when the bank's reserves
were rapidly disappearing. Of the four Kodak CEOs I was privileged to
observe, Fallon was the least impressive to me. I did, however, admire his early
recognition of the fact that RSB could not continue "business as usual" and be
able to sustain itself.

David T. Kearns   *Richard M. Eisenhart*

Joining the board in 1972, Dr. Francena L. Miller came with a special expertise in rural sociology, home economics, and social psychology. Miller earned a doctorate from Penn State University. She went on to become the dean of the Home Economics program at the University of Connecticut, and served as assistant and then executive director of the American Association of University Women from 1966 to 1968. In 1969, Miller moved to Rochester with her husband, Dr. Paul A. Miller, who had been named the president of RIT. Each year, two Paul A. and Francena L. Miller Fellowships are awarded to help RIT faculty in the College of Liberal Arts pursue scholarly and professional projects.

David Kearns joined the RSB board in 1974. Kearns was a nephew of RSB trustees Walter and George Todd. A graduate of the U of R, he roomed there with another RSB trustee, Robert Frame. From 1982 until 1990, Kearns was the CEO of Xerox. Both he and Frame said that neither of them ever dreamed that Kearns would someday head the Xerox Corporation. Kearns also served the U of R as chairman of its board of trustees. He was Deputy Secretary of the U.S. Department of Education from 1991 until 1992, and served on the Boards of the Ford Foundation and Time Warner.

Richard Eisenhart was elected to the RSB board of trustees in 1975. His father, M. Herbert Eisenhart, had been a trustee before him. The great grandson of John Jacob Bausch, founder of Bausch & Lomb, Richard Eisenhart was also an RIT trustee and served as the chair of its board for five years, from 1976 to 1981. Eisenhart has always been extremely active in RIT and community affairs.

Colby H. Chandler   *Pete C. Merrill*

Colby H. Chandler was elected to the RSB board in 1977. A University of Maine graduate and a Sloan Fellow at MIT, he went on to receive five honorary doctoral degrees. Kodak was where he "grew up," eventually serving as CEO from 1983 until 1993. Colby Chandler is a wonderful man with a very fine mind, which he sometimes tries to hide behind his great sense of humor. A Mainer, it seems that he enjoys tractors and the farm as much as he did running Kodak.

Pete C. Merrill became an RSB board member in 1979. Born in Germany, he migrated to America in 1940. Thirty-four years later, he was the CEO of B. Forman & Company, Rochester's long-time, leading ladies' apparel establishment. He was the board chair of the YMCA from 1977 to 1979.

Gene K. Shaffer   *Jessica Weis Warren*

Gene K. Shaffer, also elected in 1979, came to Rochester from the Minneapolis YMCA, in 1973, to serve as CEO of the Rochester YMCA. His trusteeship further cemented the long relationship between RSB and the YMCA. Before his arrival, the Rochester "Y" was badly in need of an update, and Shaffer turned it around. It was his idea to create what is now the Chester A. Carlson Metro Center YMCA, the downtown cornerstone of a rapidly-expanding and highly productive regional YMCA.

In 1979, Jessica ("Judy") Weis Warren was the last RSB trustee to be elected. A member of the Rochester Female Charitable Society, Warren brought full circle that organization's long-standing relationship with RSB. A trustee-emeritus of Skidmore College, in 1988 she received its alumni association's Outstanding Service Award. Warren was a champion golfer. Her mother, Judy Weis, also a Rochester Female Charitable Society member, was the first U.S. Congresswoman from New York State, and the founder, in 1923, of Rochester's famed Chatterbox Club. "Judy" Warren had a very deep Rochester taproot.

CHAPTER NINE

CONCLUDING THOUGHTS

So we come to the end of our journey–or, rather, the journey taken by a very remarkable institution. It has been quite an experience for me to uncover the history of "The Old Bank" and to find out so much about many of the remarkable individuals who were trustees. The bank and the city of Rochester were both very fortunate to have had their capable and inspired expertise. It was impossible to document all of the many contributions they made to the fabric of life in Rochester, or to mention all 153 trustees. Suffice it to say that these individuals served the bank and the community well. We are all better for their efforts and owe them a heartfelt "Thank you! Well done."

Initially, savings banks were a badly-needed safe haven for the small depositor. In general, when I reflect on the institution of the savings bank, I believe that it fulfilled its purpose well for roughly a century and a half. These banks were "good citizens," and, with their trustees, were a major force in stabilizing communities and supporting civic organizations, as well as establishing new ones. In their final decade, savings banks simply could not keep up with the rapidly-changing financial marketplace.

Mergers changed the traditional banking landscape–from one dotted with many small savings and commercial banks to huge bank conglomerates and endlessly-expanding, non-banking institutions. In short, after a very productive lifespan of 150 years, more or less, mutual savings banks ultimately became essentially redundant. The few that remain are quite often in rural areas and are not prime movers in today's huge, complicated financial world. That world has recently become overwhelmingly problematic, and ever more uncertain. It is generally acknowledged that the root cause of this is a lack of proper regulation. Savings banks were always heavily regulated, and, until the rapid growth of virtually unregulated competition in the 1980s, their viability was unquestioned.

It is hoped and assumed that the future of Citizens Bank and its parent, the Royal Bank of Scotland, will be as full of good will, good citizenship, good sense, and good business judgment as that demonstrated for 152 years by one of its oldest seminal banks, the Rochester Savings Bank.

ROCHESTER SAVINGS BANK
TIMELINE

1831–1983   Rochester Savings Bank serves the community as one
continuous, unaltered and unblemished entity for 152 years.

1831   New York State charters Rochester Savings Bank,
April 21, 1831; sixth savings bank in the state
and first chartered bank west of the Hudson River.
Created by village elders as a stabilizing influence
during chaotic growth.

Opening of the Erie Canal in 1825 triggers
population expansion to 10,000.

Organizational meeting of fifteen founding trustees
called by Dr. Levi Ward, Everard Peck and Jonathan Child
(to be Rochester's first mayor); Dr. Ward elected
first president, May 10, 1831.

David Scoville resigns as a trustee, becomes
Financial Secretary, July 1, 1831 at $300 per year;
Only employee for fifteen years.

Bank's business is conducted at a "borrowed" teller's window
on Saturday evenings; one mid-week evening monthly
"for females only."

Harmon Taylor, a grocer/baker makes first deposit of $13,
July 2, 1831.

1834–1854   *The Flour City* era consists of twenty-four mills at the falls
of the Genesee; 500,000 barrels of flour are produced per year.

1836	President Andrew Jackson shuts down the second National Bank, March 3, 1836. There would be no central United States Bank until 1913.
1837	Panic of 1837–the U.S. banking system suffers a general collapse; 343 out of 850 banks close; grain mills start to move west as railroad competition to the Erie Canal begins.
	Rochester Savings Bank remains open and continues to pay interest.
1838	New York State adopts the first comprehensive bank chartering system; requires minimum reserves to back circulating notes issued by individual banks. Minimal regulation by other states.
1842	Bank moves to its own two-story building at 47 State Street.
	Rochester population is 23,000.
1850s	Rochester Savings Bank trustees help found University of Rochester, Rochester Institute of Technology and the YMCA.
1855–1875	*The Flower City* era. The nursery and seed business is cornerstoned by the world-renowned Ellwanger & Barry Nursery.
1857	Panic of 1857. More than 5,000 American businesses fail; British investors lose confidence in U.S. banks and withdraw their money; gold pours into the economy, inflating the currency; grain prices fall when the Crimean war ends and Russia reenters the marketplace.
	Railroad land speculation ruins thousands of investors; Unregulated western banks in non-state territories issue unreserved bank notes.
	Rochester Savings Bank raises its interest rate from 5 per cent to 6 per cent; a deposit increase of 800% from 1842 forces Rochester Savings Bank to move to a new building at southwest corner of Main and Fitzhugh Streets.

1861–1865	Rochester population is 50,000.
	National Banking Act of 1863 enables nationally chartered banks to issue currency as long as it is backed by holdings in U.S. Treasury bonds, thereby establishing a national currency. RSB is a pillar of strength during the Civil War.
1873	Black Friday, Stock Market Crash, September 20, 1873; stalwart Elijah Smith serving his third term as president (1872–1880).
	Rochester Savings Bank maintains stability and deposits increase.
1874	George Eastman hired as clerk; he resigns in 1881 to start Eastman Kodak and becomes a RSB trustee in 1900.
1878	Only run on Rochester Savings Bank ends when $1,000,000 cash is displayed at the bank.
	Rochester Savings Bank adds three more floors to its two-story building at Main & Fitzhugh.
1890–1910	Rochester changes from *The Flower City* to *The City of Many Industries*.
	Rochester population is 130,000.
1893	U.S. suffers worst depression since country began and is caused by overbuilding railroads and shaky railroad financing; sets off series of bank failures, some 500 in all, mostly out west. Rochester Savings Bank survives untouched.
1907	Bankers Panic; New York Stock Exchange falls 50%; New York city banks restrict market liquidity resulting in loss of consumer confidence. J. P. Morgan helps stabilize the economy as there was no central bank and lender of last resort. Rochester Savings Bank survives untouched.

1913	Establishment of the Federal Reserve System; nationally chartered banks are required to join; state banks have the option to join, thus establishing a more orderly method of managing the nation's money supply.
1916–1919	Rochester Savings Bank establishes First School Savings Plan in City; First Payroll Savings Plan (to sell war bonds); first bank to provide free safe keeping for U.S. Bonds.
1927	First bank branch, 40 Franklin Street, features one of the finest Byzantine banking floors in America and a stunning wall mural by Ezra Winter. The building is now a national historic landmark.
1929	Stock Market Crash, October 28, 1929; Rochester Savings Bank continues paying interest as usual.
1931	Eastman Kodak Treasurer Marion Folsom Joins RSB board. He will be instrumental in writing U.S. social security legislation.
1933	The Federal Banking system collapses; newly elected President Franklin D. Roosevelt declares a Bank Holiday, Sunday March 5, 1933, closing all banks in order to determine which are solvent; Rochester's Todd Company prints two million notes-scrip–to keep Rochester afloat; banks re-open March 14, 1933; all scrip redeemed (less a few now held by collectors). Rochester Savings Bank continues paying interest as usual.
1945–1955	Rochester Savings Bank mortgage portfolio increases from $24.8 million to $107.4 million and deposits increase from $58 million to $150 million. Rochester population 332,000; the greater Rochester area–1 million. The flight to the suburbs begins; Xerox founder Joseph C. Wilson joins RSB's board in 1948.

1957	New bank building at Main & Fitzhugh Streets with first drive-up window in Rochester.
1970–1983	Great erosion of reserves caused by the run-off of deposits created by heightened competition from commercial banks and new, non-banking sources (brokerage houses, etc.); loss of reserves were also due to the bank's asset portfolio which consisted mainly of long-term, low-yielding mortgages and government bonds.
1983	Rochester Savings Bank merges with equally hard-pressed Community Savings Bank, July 1, 1983.
	The new entity, Rochester Community Savings Bank has assets of $2.4 billion and is the fifteenth largest mutual savings bank in the country.
1986	Bank charter changes from a mutual to a publically held stock institution which raises $184 million in capital.
1997	Rochester Community Savings Bank merges with Charter One Financial Corporation.
2004	Charter One Financial Corporation, with assets of $42 billion, is acquired by the Royal Bank of Scotland for $10.5 billion cash.

Crumb, Owen. *Rochester Community Savings Bank–
A Condensed Corporate History.*
Rochester, NY: Rochester Savings Bank Publications, 1997.

Federal Deposit Insurance Corporation. *The Mutual Savings Bank Crisis.
History of the Eighties — Lessons for the Future,* 1997.
http://www.fdic.gov/databank/hist80 (accessed 2004)

Gordon, Dane R. *Rochester Institute of Technology (Mellen Studies
in History).* Lewiston, NY: Edwin Mellen Press Ltd., 1982.

Hammele, Joe. "Early Banking in Rochester," 2003.

Haskins, Kenneth. *A Brief History of Rochester Savings Bank.*
Mirror. Rochester, NY: Rochester Savings Bank, 1969.

Holton, Glyn. *United States Financial Regulation,* 1996.
http://www.riskglossary.com/link/
united_states_financial_regulation.htm (accessed 2006).

McKelvey, Blake. *A Panoramic History of Rochester & Monroe.*
Woodland Hills, CA: Windsor Publications, 1979.

McKelvey, Blake. *Rochester on the Genesee: The Growth of a City.*
Syracuse, NY: Syracuse University Press, 1993.

Muhl, Gerald. "Paying For The Dreams. A Short History of Banking
in Rochester". *Rochester History.* Vol. XLIX, No. 2, 1987.

Peck, William F. *Semi-Centennial History of the City of Rochester.*
Syracuse, NY: D. Mason & Co., 1884.

Perkins, Gilman. "Be There-You'll Never Forget It". 1995.

Speare, Jack W. *In Rochester 100 Years Ago and Now:*
Centennial Year of the Rochester Savings Bank, 1831–1931.
Rochester, NY. Rochester, NY: Rochester Savings Bank Publications,
ca.1931.

Turri, Susan T. *The Rochester Savings Bank, 1831–1981.*
Rochester, NY: Monroe Litho Inc., 1981.

Upstate Business Journal. "Harris Beach Law Firm History."
July 7, 2006, pp. 21–32,

Sources

Central Library of Rochester and Monroe County, Rochester, NY. Publications and photographs.

City of Rochester, Photographic Collection.

George Eastman House, Rochester, NY.

Kodak Historical Collection No. 003/Department of Rare Books Special Collections and Preservation, Rush Rhees Library, University of Rochester, Rochester, NY.

Landmark Society, 2005. Various tours.

Local History Division. Central Library of Rochester and Monroe County, Rochester, NY. Publications, photographs and websites.

Melbert B. Cary, Jr. Graphic Arts Collection, Rochester Institute of Technology, Rochester, NY.

Rare Books, Special Collections & Preservation, Rush Rhees Library, University of Rochester, Rochester, NY. Publications and photographs.

Rochester Historical Society. Photographs and documents.

RIT Institute of Fellows, 2003.

Rochester Museum and Science Center. Libraries and Collections Department. 1873 Rochester Time Capsule under cornerstone of Rochester Savings Bank building. Case IV, Drawer A, Item No. 2 http://collections.rmsc.org/index.html (accessed December 19, 2005).

RSB Archives, author's personal collection.

Presidents of Rochester Savings Bank

Levi Ward, Jr.	June 13, 1831	to	January 19, 1842
William Pitkin	February 16, 1842	to	March 1, 1849
Jacob Gould	March 1, 1849	to	May 20, 1850
Elijah F. Smith	May 20, 1850	to	February 1, 1858
John Haywood	February 1, 1858	to	February 7, 1859
Elijah F. Smith	February 7, 1859	to	February 6, 1860
William Kidd	February 6, 1860	to	February 6, 1865
George H. Mumford	February 6, 1865	to	October 2, 1865
William A. Reynolds	December 4, 1865	to	January 12, 1872
Elijah F. Smith	February 3, 1872	to	February 2, 1880
Isaac Hills	February 2, 1880	to	October 10, 1881
Mortimer F. Reynolds	February 6, 1882	to	June 13, 1892
James Brackett	July 8, 1892	to	March 7, 1904
Hobart F. Atkinson	June 6, 1904	to	August 14, 1908
Harold P. Brewster	February 1, 1908	to	February 1, 1923
Henry S. Hanford	February 1, 1923	to	January 12, 1927
Edwin Allen Stebbins	February 7, 1927	to	February 15, 1951
Thomas H. Hawks	February 15, 1951	to	April 13, 1970
F. Stanley DeVoy	April 13, 1970	to	July 15, 1971
Frederick G. Ray	July 15, 1971	to	July 1, 1983

Index

H

Haloid Company, 69
Hanford, Henry, 60, 82
Hargrave, Thomas J., 70
Harriet Hollister Spencer
   Memorial State Recreation Area, 65
Harris, Albert, 50, 59
Harris, Edward, 41, 50, 59, 65
Harris, Edward Jr., 59, 70, 71
Harris, Elizabeth, 50, 59
Harris, Haven, Beach & Harris
   law firm, 59
Harris, Richard M., 65
Harris Beach law firm, 41, 59, 74
Harris Home, 41
Harris & Ives law firm, 41
Hart, Roswell, 37
Harvard University,
   57, 62, 64, 66, 68, 71, 75, 81
Hawks, Marion, 66
Hawks, Thomas Harris,
   53, 65, 66, 70, 71, 72, 74, 77
Hayden Company, 51
Hervey Ely house, 17
Hill, Charles J., 27
Hill Flour, 27
Hills, Isaac, 25, 57
Hillside Children's Center, 20, 43
Hochstein Music School, 49
Hollister, Emmett, 39
Hollister, Granger, 65
Hollister, Harriet, 65
Hollister House, 39
Hollister Lumber Company, 39, 55, 65
Home for the Friendless, 20
Hopeman, Albert A., 62
Howe, Ernest J., 78
HSBC 18, 51

I

Industrial School of Rochester, 20
International Baseball League, 48
Ives, Henry, 41

J

Jackson, Andrew, 25, 27
Johnson, Lyndon, 74
Jonathan Child House, 23
Joseph C. Wilson Health Center, 70
J.P. Morgan Chase Bank,
   18, 48, 51, 57, 65

K

Kearns, David T., 70, 85
Kempshall, Thomas, 36, 38
Kempshall, Willis, 36
KeyBank, 18
Kidd, William, 17, 33
Kimball, William S., 45, 46
Kimball Tobacco Company, 44, 45

L

Langie, Louis A., 77
Langie Fuel Service, Inc., 77
Lee, William E., 80, 81
Lincoln Alliance Bank Group, 51, 57
Lincoln Rochester Bank, 65
Linowitz, Sol, 70, 73, 74
Livingston Park, 17
Longworth, Alice Roosevelt, 75

R

COLOPHON

Author	James C. Duffus
Design	Bruce Ian Meader
Editor	Molly Q. Cort
Production	IBT Global
Typefaces	Garamond designed by Claude Garamond
	Copperplate Gothic Bold designed by Frederic W. Goudy
	and Neutraface 2 Text designed by Christian Schwartz
Photography	Cover photography by Ken Haskins, Rochester Savings Bank

The following photographs are courtesy
"from the collection of the Rochester Public Library,
Local History Division:"

Abelard Reynolds	Genesee Falls
Addison Gardiner	Mortimer Reynolds House
James G. Cutler	William Kimball
Rochester Driving Park	Kimball Tobacco Company

The photograph of Hiram Watson Sibley is courtesy of the
Ruth T. Watanabe Special Collections, Sibley Music Library,
Eastman School of Music, University of Rochester.

The photographs of Rufus Sibley and Thomas Finucane are
courtesy of the Rochester Historical Society.

The images of the former Rochester mayors and
photographs from the historical collection are courtesy of the
City of Rochester, New York.